T0349964

OCTOBER 16, 1943

∎ ∎ ∎ ∎ ∎ ∎ ∎ ∎

EIGHT JEWS

OCTOBER 16, 1943

■ ■ ■ ■ ■ ■ ■ ■

EIGHT JEWS

Giacomo Debenedetti

Translated by
Estelle Gilson
With a Preface by
Alberto Moravia

University of Notre Dame Press
Notre Dame, Indiana

Translated by Estelle Gilson from the Italian edition entitled *16 ottobre
1943* 1993 © Sellerio, Palermo.

© 2001 Giulio Einaudi editore S.p.A.

The publisher gratefully acknowledges permission from the Centro di
Cultura Ebraica, Rome, to reproduce the book stamps which appear in the
publication *Shalom*.

Library of Congress Cataloging-in-Publication Data
Debenedetti, Giacomo, 1901–1967.
    [16 ottobre 1943. English]
October 16, 1943 ; Eight Jews / Giacomo Debenedetti ;
translated by Estelle Gilson ; with a preface by Alberto Moravia.

        p. cm.
    ISBN 0-268-03713-2 (cloth : alk. paper)
    1. Debenedetti, Giacomo, 1901–1967. 2. Jews—
Persecutions—Italy—Rome. 3. Ardeatine Massacre, 1944—
Personal narratives. 4. Holocaust, Jewish (1939–1945)—Italy—Rome—
Personal narratives. 5. Rome (Italy)—Ethnic relations.
I. Gilson, Estelle. II. Debenedetti, Giacomo, 1901–1967. Otto ebrei.
English. III. Title. IV. Title: October 16, 1943 ; Eight Jews. V. Title:
October sixteen, nineteen forty three. VI. Title: Eight Jews.
DS135.I85R62413   2001
940.53'18'0945—dc21

2001003527

Contents

■ ■ ■ ■ ■ ■ ■ ■ ■ ■ ■

Translator's
Acknowledgments

∎ ∎ ∎ ∎ ∎ ∎ ∎ ∎ ∎ ∎ ∎

I would like to thank the many people here and abroad whose various and unique contributions helped shape this work. In the United States they are Fanny Peczenik, who called my attention to the fact that the Roman Jewish community library was still missing, Susan Zuccotti, who supported my early interest in the project, and Benton Arnovitz, Director of Academic Publications, United States Holocaust Memorial Museum, who pointed me in all the right directions. I also owe a debt to Jeffrey L. Gainey, associate director of the University of Notre Dame Press, for his immediate and sustained enthusiasm for this work and to my editor, John McCudden, whose practiced eye saved me embarrassments. Bice Migliau, director of the Centro di Cultura Ebraica (Jewish Cultural Center) and Antonio Debenedetti, son of the late Giacomo Debenedetti, were generous with their time in Rome and replied patiently to many subsequent inquiries. Benjamin Richler, director of Jerusalem's Institute of Microfilmed Hebrew

Translator's Acknowledgments

Manuscripts answered a stream of e-mail inquiries with remarkable candor and alacrity. And Astrid M. Eckert, of the Free University of Berlin, of whom I made a general inquiry, responded beyond any expectation with invaluable assistance and advice.

I am indebted, too, to the Memorial Foundation for Jewish Culture and to the Littauer Foundation for grants which enabled this work to go forward.

OCTOBER 16, 1943

■ ■ ■ ■ ■ ■ ■ ■

EIGHT JEWS

Translator's Introduction

■　■　■　■　■　■　■　■　■　■　■

For more than fifty years Giacomo Debenedetti's *October 16, 1943*, an account of one of the most shockingly brief and efficient roundups of the Holocaust—the seizure of over a thousand Roman Jews for the gas chambers of Auschwitz—has been recognized as a literary classic. Completed a year after the event, filled with intimate details and vivid glimpses into the lives of its victims, the work has served every historian of the period. *Eight Jews*, its companion piece, was written in response to testimony about the Ardeatine Cave Massacres of March 24, 1944. In it Debenedetti offers insights into that grisly horror and an unusual concept of racial equality. These two brief works give American readers a first glimpse into the extraordinary mind of the man who was Italy's foremost critic of twentieth-century literature.

Giacomo Debenedetti (1901–67) was born to an observant Jewish family in Biella in Northern Italy, close to the Swiss and French frontiers. He was brought

1

up and educated in Turin. Committed early to literature as a profession, by age twenty he had founded a literary review called *Primo Tempo* and went on to edit other publications, to publish a collection of short fiction (*Amedeo and Other Stories*) and to write cinema scripts, film and music reviews. In 1937 Debenedetti moved his family to Rome. When the Nazis occupied the city in 1943, though Debenedetti's wife was Catholic, the entire family was forced into hiding in Cortona. After the war he resumed his own critical work and was an editor at the Italian publishing house of Mondadori.

Though Debenedetti taught at the Universities of Messina and Rome, he never held a university chair. Inasmuch as many Jews held university posts until passage of the racial laws in 1938 and again after the war, neither race nor religion was likely the factor that kept Debenedetti from such a position. Most likely Debenedetti himself was. Described as "part scholar, part rabbi, part dandy," Debenedetti, who hobnobbed with the leading leftist intellectuals of his time, among them Jean-Paul Sartre and Pablo Neruda, was nevertheless too politically and methodologically heterodox, too nonconformist to fit comfortably into any ideological or administrative scheme of things. In *Giacomino*, a memoir, his son Antonio Debenedetti recalls that his "venerated and somewhat mysterious father didn't return to life until 1 in the afternoon" and then it would take a terrifying hour or two before his waking wrath subsided and he once again became "the irresistible conversationalist and middle-European charmer" he had been in some anti-Fascist home or restaurant the night before. Early on, Debenedetti, who believed that fiction was the lifeblood of modern literature, became a champion of then unknown writers Italo Svevo, Umberto Saba, and Marcel Proust. (He was in fact engaged in translating Proust into Italian during the time he was in hiding in 1943 and 1944). Is it significant that these three writers were Jewish? It would seem so in light of the fact that, as Alberto Moravia points out in his Preface, no one would have expected this assimilated, leftist, detached literary critic to write about the horrors visited on Roman Jewry, and to do so, so movingly. Svevo, Saba, and Proust were writing with new and strange personal sensitivities of the outsider—the emancipated-but-never-included Jew. All wanted passionately to be involved in chosen worlds to which they did not belong—Proust and Saba, for reasons that went beyond their Jewishness. As for Debenedetti's Jewishness, though it may have lain dormant for years, when called upon, as we will see in *Eight Jews*, its voice rose in him like thunder.

October 16, 1943 and *Eight Jews* were completed within a month of each other. Each reflects Debenedetti's reaction to an outrage against Jews, but the two works are very different in tone. *October 16, 1943* is an essentially factual account of the events of that day, and those immediately leading up to and following it. Debenedetti completed it in November 1944. He completed *Eight Jews* in September 1944, though the event that triggered that passionate work had taken place only days before. *October 16, 1943* begins with a lyrical passage in praise of the Sabbath and speaks of peace and openness. *Eight Jews* begins *in medias res* and speaks of impending death. At the conclusion of

October 16, 1943 Debenedetti asks only silence of his readers. *Eight Jews* concludes on a note that would create argument in any assemblage, Jewish or not. Though the style, intent, and effect of these two works are so different, the works themselves share a characteristic which, perhaps, only those of us reading (and translating?) half a century after they were written can perceive: a sense of intimacy. The war was not yet over when Debenedetti completed these pieces. The Germans had fled Rome, but their concentration camps, gas chambers, and crematories raged on, and the atrocities they had committed within the city were still being uncovered. Surviving Italians (Jews and non-Jews) were inhabiting a nightmare that was not yet over. In writing to and for them, it was as if Debenedetti were writing to and for family. Rarely did directness have to give way to explanatory detours. No need to explain who Badoglio was, or Caruso, or that via Tasso was to be read as Gestapo headquarters. The quality of transparency that Italian writer Natalia Ginzburg, a contemporary of Debenedetti's, extolled in these pieces owes much to the shared experiences which bound all Italians, including this usually detached literary critic, at that particular moment.

The Roman Jewish community is the oldest Jewish community in the world. The first record of Jews in Rome appears in 161 B.C. After the Roman invasion of Judea in 63 B.C., and again after the destruction of the Temple in Jerusalem in 70 A.D., Jews were brought back to Rome as slaves. There are families in Italy today who trace their lineage to these distant ancestors. About 2,000 Jews were living in the low-lying area along the Tiber River known as the Ghetto when Pope Paul IV walled it off in 1555. With brief respites the walls remained in place until the unification of Italy in 1870. Mussolini came to power in 1922. The racial laws were passed in 1938. Rome's Jews had only sixty-eight years—one lifetime of relative freedom after more than three hundred years in the Ghetto—before the Holocaust was upon them. Most were still living within its confines.

October 16, 1943, was a Sabbath—entire families were sure to be at home. Debenedetti begins his story on the evening before, when soon after the appearance of the evening star that signals the onset of the holy day, an unkempt woman brings the alarm that no one heeds.

Soon we learn of the previous insults and outrages perpetrated against the Jewish community, including the demand for gold, the seizure of its libraries (about which more later), and of the lists of Jewish names that the Germans laboriously collected, and we wonder, as Debenedetti did, that not one word of the impending raid ever reached the Ghetto.

Word, however, had reached Allied intelligence units.

On June 26, 2000, the National Archives and Records Administration (NARA) in Washington, D.C., made available approximately 400,000 pages of previously classified documents of the Office of Strategic Services, wartime precursor of the CIA. These include radioed messages between Rome and Berlin during the summer and fall of 1943 which British intelligence units had intercepted and deciphered. It is clear from these documents that both British and American authorities were aware of the ongoing

5

Holocaust and had advance knowledge of the planned roundup of Rome's Jews.

Here is a brief summary of events in Italy prior to the roundup and excerpts from some intercepted messages.

Summer 1943: Italy's dictator, Benito Mussolini, is overthrown and imprisoned on July 25. A new government headed by Pietro Badoglio is established. An Allied landing in Italy is thought to be imminent. Italians, Romans in particular, are euphoric. Anti-Fascists hiding elsewhere in the country begin returning to the city, and its Jews feel safer than they have for many years. But Badoglio does not repeal the racial laws, and the answer to Debenedetti's oft-asked question about how the Germans knew exactly where to find Jews, says historian Susan Zuccotti, is that "Badoglio's bureaucrats refused to destroy their many lists of Jewish names and addresses. Nearly all these fell into German hands."

September 3: Allied troops land in Calabria.

September 8: Though the troops are nowhere near Rome, the Badoglio government surrenders to the Allies.

September 10: German forces from Northern Italy enter Rome and Badoglio flees.

September 12: Germans rescue Mussolini to reestablish him in the north. The radioed message to Berlin on the 12th, which reads in part, "MUSSOLINI [*sic*] undertaking succeeded," is signed by Major Herbert Kappler. Kappler, who, with his aide, Captain Kurt Schutz, is mentioned only briefly by Debenedetti in connection with the extortion of gold from the Jewish community, was head of the Gestapo in Rome. An Italophile, Kappler is said to have loved the city so much that he had his parents join him there. He and

Schutz played major roles in both the roundup and the seizure of victims for the Ardeatine Cave Massacres.

September 16: Additional German forces arrive in Rome. The city is completely under German control.

October 5: Kappler radios Berlin to report the removal "of 110 tons of Italian State gold to Milan" and "50kgs of gold from Jews in Rome."

October 6: Kappler receives a message reading "hearty congratulations on promotion and on the Iron Cross."

On this day too, the doom of Roman Jews and the good fortune of Neapolitan Jews becomes known to the Allies. A message to Berlin reads, "SS Ogruf WOLFF RSHA has sent SS Hptstuf. Dannecker to this end with order to seize all Jews in lightning actions and to forward them to GERMANY. Because of the attitude in the town and uncertain conditions, action could not be carried through in NAPLES. Office preparations for action in ROME have been concluded." Other messages on this day report on plans to "remove," "arrest," and/or "disarm" various elements of the Italian armed forces, including the carabinieri.

October 11: Kappler is told, "It is precisely the immediate and thorough eradication of the Jews in ITALY which is/the [*sic*] special interest of the present internal political situation and the general security in ITALY. To postpone the expulsion of the Jews until the CARABINIERI and the Italian army officers have been removed can no more be considered than the idea mentioned of calling up the Jews in ITALY for what would probably be very improductive [*sic*] labour under responsible direction of Italian authorities."

Historians will have much to study in this recently released material. Some who have already dealt with these documents speculate that a warning was withheld to protect the fact that the German code had been compromised. Yet as Debenedetti's and other accounts make clear, Roman Jews were ambivalent—trapped between fears for their lives based on the little they knew and all that they had heard about Nazi atrocities, and the human desire to overcome such overwhelming fears, which surely at times must have seemed as exaggerated and irrational as the fears one suffers at a horror film. As historian Timothy Naftali suggested in introducing these documents to the public, perhaps British Prime Minister Winston Churchill or American President Franklin Roosevelt should have made a statement warning the Jews. A hint—a feather of a word from a high and trusted source that made it clear that the nightmarish fears were indeed real might have tipped the balance for more than a thousand souls.

October 16: Rome's message to Berlin at the end of this day is a steely contrast to Debenedetti's account. "Action against Jews started and finished today in accordance with a plan worked out as well as possible by office. All available forces of the Sicherseitspol, and the Ordnungspol. employed. Participation of the Italian police was not possible in view of unreliability in this respect, as only possible by individual arrests in quick succession inside the 26 action districts. To cordon off whole blocks of streets, in view both of [Rome's] character as an open city and of the insufficient number of German police, 365 in all, not practicable. In spite of this 1259 persons were arrested in Jewish homes and taken to assembly camp[s] of the military school here in the course of the action which lasted from 0530 to 1400 hours. After the release of those of mixed blood, of foreigners including a Vatican citizen, of the families in mixed marriages including the Jewish partner, and of the Aryan servants and lodgers, there remained 1002 Jews to be detained. Transportation on Monday 1/?/10 [*sic*] at 0900. Escort by 30 men (?) [*sic*] of the Ordnungspolizei (?) [*sic*] Attitude of the Italian population was unequivocally one of passive resistance, which in a large number of individual cases has developed into active assistance. . . . part of the population did not make an appearance during the action but only the broad masses, who in individual cases even attempted to keep single policemen back from the Jews."

October 20: Berlin is informed of the departure of the sealed train. "Transport of Jews from ROME left ROME on 18th at 0900 hours with transport No. X70469 and is traveling via ARNOLDSTEIN to AUSCHWITZ."

The figure of those actually deported on the Rome-Auschwitz transport varies, though not widely. All authorities agree it was higher than Kappler's figure. The highest figure, 1,056, was cited by Robert Katz in his *Black Sabbath,* a book-length account of the events surrounding the roundup. Katz lists the names of the deported as well as the names of fifteen who survived to return to Rome. *The Encyclopedia of the Holocaust* states that 1,035 people were on the train. In *La Parola Ebreo,* Italian writer Rosetta Loy states that 1,023 people were deported on October 16 and that seventeen returned. During the eight months that the German occupation of Rome continued, Loy writes, 723 other Jews were arrested; 75 of them were shot in the Ardeatine Caves, 4 were killed elsewhere, and the remaining 644 were sent to Auschwitz. The oldest person to die in the Caves was seventy-four-year-old Moisè Di Consiglio, born in 1870, the year the Ghetto doors were opened.

"Rome, March 24, 1944. They are working on the so-called preliminary list for the Ardeatine Caves. The Germans, on their own, have already taken ten hostages."

Italians reading these first lines of *Eight Jews* in September 1944 understood every ugly nuance of their meaning.

When, in September 1943, Badoglio fled the city, he left no orders for Italian armed forces or police on how to respond to the Germans. And when, a month later, on October 13, he declared war on Germany, the only Italy he represented was the area south of Rome occupied by the Allies. Thousands of Italian troops in German-controlled territory were captured or killed. Many of those who survived fled with whatever arms and equipment they could carry away, to become partisans.

On March 23, 1944, a partisan unit exploded a bomb in via Rasella, a narrow street in the center of Rome, which housed a German SS patrol. Twenty-six Germans died instantly, five shortly thereafter. Hitler ordered ten Italians killed for every German within twenty-four hours.

Immediately German SS and the Italian Fascist police began selecting three hundred and ten "candidates for death" from among "persons condemned to death or life imprisonment, and prisoners not yet judged, but guilty of crimes punishable on pain of death." On the German side Herbert Kappler was in charge of the entire operation. Kurt Schutz was in charge of planning the executions. The head of the Italian operation was Questore (Police Commissioner) Pietro Caruso, a longtime Fascist, who had taken office only a month earlier. Raffaele Alianello, who spoke the two sentences that begin *Eight Jews* was Rome's chief of public security.

Germans and Italians worked separately and frenetically on the lists. There weren't enough prisoners as defined by the original order to satisfy their needs. People were chosen indiscriminately. When another wounded German died, Kappler added ten more names to his list. At one point the Germans backed a truck up to Rome's Regina Coeli prison and according to one account, took the first men they saw, some of whom had just been acquitted of charges and were awaiting the return of their belongings. Caruso left the final paring of his list to Alianello and prison director Donato Carretta.

By the time the names were chosen and the German engineers had prepared the Ardeatine Caves—the site selected for the executions—Kappler was pressed for time. He could not allow more than one shot and one minute for each man. The men, tied together in fives, were taken into the caves and told to kneel with their heads up, facing a wall. They were shot in the head at an angle that assured instant death. Then the next five were brought in. Each group of bodies was piled on the one before. The caves were deep and dark. The work was done by lantern light. After some hours a German lieutenant rebelled against the horror. Kappler enticed him back to work. Eventually

335 men were killed—doctors, peddlers, diplomats, store-keepers, a boy of fifteen, even a priest—and the entrance to the cave was blown up. But the stench of death soon revealed the location of the bodies. And just in case Rome was slow to comprehend the meaning of the massacre, its citizens were put on notice of the price of resistance at a press conference.

"I told Carretta to take ten names off. Eight Jewish names were at the very end of it. We figured they'd been added at the last minute in order to get the total to fifty. So Carretta took them off along with two other names we chose at random."

These are the next words spoken by Raffaele Alianello in his own and Caruso's defense—the words which infuriated Debenedetti and sparked the writing of *Eight Jews*. To Debenedetti, Alianello's decision to remove eight Jewish names from the list of the doomed solely because they were Jewish, and Jews had already suffered much, was as prejudicial an act as adding Jewish names to a list of the doomed would have been. Equality, to Debenedetti, meant that there were not to be any favors, preferences, or recompense for past sufferings. Alianello asserted he had crossed off two Italian names at random. In not intermixing Jewish and non-Jewish names, then choosing by lot from that list, he had not, in Debenedetti's mind, granted Jews equality with Italians.

Compounding what Debenedetti considered this prejudicial act, Alianello sought credit for it. Debenedetti writes scathingly of Alianello's duplicitous attempt to use the act to earn him consideration as an anti-Fascist, seeking to make of Jews—the very people he had helped destroy—witnesses in behalf of a new evil and unprincipled scheme to save himself and Caruso.

Debenedetti's theses that Alianello had been at fault in crossing off the Jewish names and that equality demands there be no special treatment even in recompense for past injustice, were not well received in Italy when *Eight Jews* was published. Presented today, these ideas would likely evoke outright hostility in a society grown accustomed to lawsuits and demands for recompense for all who claim past injury.

More surprising than the fact that this literary critic, who no longer practiced his religion, would write so powerfully about the Holocaust, is the fact that he so unabashedly assumed the mantle of spokesman for all Jews in *Eight Jews*. In it he writes, "There is no denying that there are deep internal and individual ways of feeling oneself Jewish. But these are private feelings, bounded by a sense of modesty, and never publicly demonstrated by deed." Only recently, a clue to the depth and nature of Debenedetti's private feelings emerged with the discovery of his youthful, powerful identification with the prophets of Israel. In 1924, when he was only twenty-three years of age, he created a series of five lectures on the Prophets, which he delivered to the Jewish community in Turin. So important were they to him that he wrote to Umberto Saba asking to arrange for him to give his lectures to young Jews in Trieste. The newly discovered notes for this lecture series were published in 1998 in Italy under the title of *Profeti*.

In February 2001, the city of Rome celebrated the centenary of Debenedetti's birth, with a four-day conference devoted to the study of his life and works.

Alberto Moravia's Preface to *October 16, 1943*

In 1938, absurdity, always present under dictatorships, entered my life decisively with passage of the so-called laws for the defense of the race. My father was Jewish, but my mother, whose name was de Marsanich, was not, and we children had been baptized. Absurdity, therefore took the name of *"exclusion."* As my father's children, we were Jews, and as my mother's, Aryans, and moreover baptized. We were *excluded*, that is, absolved in a way, because of insufficient evidence, of the crime of injuring the race by our birth. That wasn't enough, however. Absurdity required that three years later, my brother, a lieutenant in the engineers in Africa, be blown up by a mine, and die in a war that had erupted precisely to impose that same absurdity on the entire world. Still not enough. Again, because of absurdity, my mother began taking steps toward changing our *Jewish* name to an *Aryan* one—the name of my maternal grandmother. When I objected, my mother, with good sense, answered that in such dire predicaments one name was as good as any other. Of course! Finally, excluded but always suspect, I was prohibited from signing my own name in newspapers. I then took the transparent pseudonym of Pseudo. All of this by way of saying that in those years, for reasons wholly connected with Fascism, my identity daily became more uncertain, more problematic, more ephemeral.

Fascism fell, the Badoglio period followed, I wrote articles critical of the fallen regime in *Popolo di Roma,* edited by Corrado Alvaro. After that came the 8th of September, Nazis and Fascists returned. And then I began to see that absurdity, after having been a kind of agonizing limbo for a long time, was now becoming the hell which in truth it was. In other words, I began to feel the emotion of fear, which under regimes of terror strikes all those who, for whatever reasons, are not, or do not feel themselves to be, "in conformity." In no way was I in conformity, not racially, politically, nor culturally. On the other hand, even had I wanted to, I couldn't be in conformity. I couldn't invent an Aryan grandfather, I couldn't believe in Fascism, and lastly, I could not not write in the style in which I was writing. I was, in short, irremediably "different."

One morning, walking through the Piazza di Spagna, I met a foreign journalist, a member of the foreign press corps, who warned me that I was on the list of those who very shortly would be arrested and sent to Germany. Immediately I went back home and told my wife that we had to get out as quickly as we could. As I was packing a suitcase with the necessities for our flight, the telephone rang. I lifted the receiver, put it to my ear, and heard a not exactly friendly voice ask, "Am I speaking to the traitor Moravia?" Thus "different," in a few days I had become "traitor"! But that was right too.

It is not important here to tell how I got through all that. What I really would like to try to explain is the nature of the ever deepening, more anguished feeling of apprehension that I experienced in those days. I've described it as the feeling that those who know, or fear, they are not "in conformity," suffer in regimes of terror. But what exactly is terror? In my opinion, at least in the light of that far-past experience, terror consists in the disintegration of the institutions which form the foundation of our identity, and in the painful and very difficult replacement of identity with the anonymous and undifferentiated instinct of self-preservation. In short, I felt like a trapped animal, and like a trapped animal, I no longer felt I was a person, an individual, a man; rather a lump of threatened existence. If I had had time and an inclination to reflection, I would certainly have recognized in that diminuition of my identity to a mere biological datum a forced regression to a natural state. In fact, terror is the normal state in nature. For example, the herds of zebras that one so often sees browsing tranquilly and serenely in Africa, are in fact, "terrified." At the slightest indication of danger, the entire herd will gallop away en masse. Man has tried to eliminate terror—the natural condition—through the creation of institutions. The failure of institutions creates absurdity, which in turn, plunges incredulous, horrified man back into nature's ancient terror.

Why do I introduce this autobiographical note to the preface to Giacomo Debenedetti's *October 16, 1943*?

Because as I prepare to speak about the Nazis' roundup of Roman Jews, it occurs to me that I would be dishonest if I hid the fact that I too have known terror, that I too have gone through the ordeal of the collapse of institutions, of the disappearance of identity, and of the relapse, however briefly, into a natural state. I too, in short, have known persecution, meaning active and zealous injustice. So, I say again, it would be less than honest to hide it, and to pretend, in writing this preface, to an "above the fray" serenity. Though twenty-five years have passed, it would, in a way, be tantamount to denying my solidarity with those unfortunate souls whom Kappler's SS troops arrested that long-distant morning and sent to their deaths in the crematoria of the extermination camps.

Giacomo Debenedetti's little book is intended as a moving and precise account of that terrible morning. But we have to be clear about the nature of the book. The introductory note to the Saggiatore edition compares *October 16, 1943* to Manzoni's *Column of Infamy* and Defoe's *A Journal of the Plague Year*. The comparison can be sustained primarily with reference to the substance of the book. Analogous to Defoe and Manzoni, Debenedetti describes a public calamity as unimaginable and unpredictable as it was undeserved. The plague, Defoe's and Manzoni's subject, becomes ideology in Debenedetti. The resemblance between disease and ideology, both of them irresistible and rapidly propagated, has been described by more than one writer. It will suffice here to recall *The Plague* by Camus and the story called *The Epidemic* by the undersigned. On the other hand, the felicitous balance of elements in Debenedetti's account constitutes another point of resemblance with the Defoe and Manzoni works. But the comparisons, in my opinion, must end here. Debenedetti was not a puritan realist like Defoe, nor a Catholic moralist like Manzoni. He wasn't even a storyteller, as both of them were. He was a critic, who belonged by right to a European culture that straddled two centuries. A decadent culture from a historical point of view—the least one can say of it is that it was absolutely unprepared to cope with the tragedies of those past years. Debenedetti's very preference for Proust is significant. Proust does not exist outside of institutions. He is a "protected" writer, who has certainly subjected identities to original and relentless analysis, but never questioned them. Perhaps, actually, *past* and *memory* in Proust could have been interpreted as flight presaged by *terror* which lay hidden in the present and even more, in the immediate future. In short, no one was less suited than Debenedetti to describe the fate of Roman Jews, that is, the collapse of institutions and the substitution of terror for identity.

But no. The subtle, the sophisticated, the intellectual Debenedetti, in the fifty brief pages of *October 16, 1943,* succeeds in giving us everything we might have expected from a writer of Defoe and Manzoni's ilk. Reason shocked in the face of irrational fury, religious charity, historical compassion, existential torment. But how did this all come about?

In the first place, thanks to literature, Debenedetti must have understood that he could not expect any help from intellectual and psychological decadence and turned instead to the classics as his only possible model. However, the most interesting aspect of this literary effort is that

Debenedetti resorted to the classicism of a refined intellectual such as he himself was; that is, he told the story of the Nazi roundup in a style lightly coated with estheticism. In other words, at the same moment that Debenedetti was freeing himself from his own intellectualism, he was confirming it in the very way he chose to free himself of it. At this point, someone might ask "Why estheticism?" I reply, why is there art in the tomb? Estheticism. In this case, it means compassion.

But estheticism could not suffice. Pain was also required. Does a critic suffer? Does he enter into the world's suffering? I doubt it. Above all, and unavoidably, literature forms a barrier between him and suffering. Now Debenedetti has had the courage to knock down the barrier and to accept his own suffering as the principle motive for his writing. Thus we must view the little book as a victory of pain over literature. A difficult victory that allowed literature to mingle with pain and to confer upon it the elevated status of tragedy.

On the subject of the Nazi roundup there is little I can say that Debenedetti has not already said very well. I would like to add only that Debenedetti touched upon the truly painful point of the whole sinister business in these pages precisely through his rediscovery of the classically balanced approach. Racism is a mass ideology, and its victims neither have, nor can be allowed to have, individual and recognizable faces; they too are seen as a mass. The pain, therefore, is not merely about the injustice but also about the crumbling of humanistic values, the end of the interval of individualism between primitive barbarity and the barbarity yet to come.

October 16, 1943

▪ ▪ ▪ ▪ ▪ ▪ ▪ ▪ ▪ ▪ ▪

Until a few weeks ago, on Friday evenings, at the appearance of the first star, the great doors of the synagogue, those facing the Temple Square, would be opened wide. Why the great doors, instead of the less conspicuous entry at the side, as on all other nights? Why, instead of the narrow seven-branched candlesticks, so many blazing lights, which drew flames from all that was gold, radiance from plaster carvings—stars of David, Solomon knots, and Jubilee trumpets—and lustrous flashes from the brocaded curtain hung before the holy Ark, the ark of the Covenant with the Lord? Because every Friday evening at the appearance of the first star, the return of the Sabbath was celebrated.

Not the thin psalmody of the cantor, lost at the distant altar, but from the choir stall above, amid the resounding praises of the organ, the chorus of young voices raised high in a song of holy love; the old kabbalists' hymn, *Lekhah dodi, likrat Kallah,* "Come, my beloved, come to meet the Sabbath." It was the mystical invitation to greet the approaching Sabbath, the Sabbath that arrives like a bride.

But it was a disheveled, dirty woman dressed all in black, who arrived in the old Roman ghetto that Friday evening, the 15th of October. Drenched in rain, she can hardly speak, agitation chokes back her words, spittle forms at her mouth. She has run all the way from Trastevere. Just a while ago, at the home of a woman for whom she cleans half days, she'd met a woman, a carabiniere's wife, who told her that the carabiniere had run into a German, and that the German had a list of two hundred Jewish heads of households, who, with their entire families, were going to be deported.

The Jews of the Regola quarter were still in the habit of going to sleep early. Shortly after dark they were all in their homes. Perhaps the memory of an ancient curfew is still in their blood; from the time, when at the first fall of shadow, the gates of the ghetto screeched shut with an inviolable monotony that routine had perhaps rendered gentle and familiar to them, a reminder that night was not a time for Jews; that at night they were in danger of being seized, taxed, fined, imprisoned, beaten. Thus, those Jews accused of plotting in the shadows against world peace and security have in reality for ages been diurnal creatures. From early morning, just after the barest gleam of light, thick and gray as their houses, begins to rise up to the cornices, and like a can opener inserts its spiral corkscrew down into the alleys below, you'll find all these Jews out on the street shouting, calling out each other's names, agreeing, arguing, discussing, setting up trades and deals, carrying on at great length despite the fact that their discussions and transactions may have no great urgency. But these Jews love life; and their need for it, which night denies them, bursts through.

On that evening as well, families were already gathered in their homes. Mothers were lighting candles in Sabbath candlesticks—not the best ones, which had been hidden since the first German plundering—while old men with *tephila*[1] prayer books in their laps were reciting the blessings and alternating between mumbling prayers and hoarse and angry tirades against their noisy grandchildren. So the disheveled woman had no difficulty assembling a large group of Jews to warn of the danger.

But no one would believe it. They all laughed at the idea. Even though she lives in Trastevere, Celeste has relatives here, in the Ghetto, and is well known to the entire *Kehila*.[2] Everyone knows she's a gossipmonger, a hysteric, crazy. It's enough to see her gesticulate as she talks, with her wild eyes and that bird's nest hair. And besides, it's a fact that everyone in her family is a little touched. Who doesn't know her oldest son, the one who's twenty-four, thin, hairy, dark and weird, who looks like a *haham*[3] manqué, and who they even say has epilepsy? How can anyone pay attention to Celeste?

"You have to believe me. Get away, I'm telling you," the woman pleaded. "I swear it's the truth, on my children's heads."

---

1. Formulary of prayers. (Notes marked with an asterisk are the translator's.)
2. Community.
3. Learned, sage; and, by extension, rabbi.

The truth? Who knows what anyone might have said to her? Who knows what she understood? Their laughter, their disbelief, infuriates her. She begins to lose her temper, to use foul language—it's as if she, not the Germans, is their primary threat, and now she feels insulted at not being treated seriously. If she knew how to do it, she would carry on even more, to avenge herself and to finally instill some fear. She shouts, implores, her eyes fill with tears, she sets her hands on the heads of little ones as if she is there to protect them.

"You'll be sorry. If I were a fancy lady, you would believe me! But because I don't have a penny, because I'm wearing these rags . . ." and in pulling at her clothes in fury, she tears them all the more.

By now thirteen months have passed, and many who witnessed that evening are inclined to acknowledge that perhaps, if Celeste had been a lady, and not the poor wretch that she is. . . . Nevertheless on that evening, they returned home, resumed sitting around their tables, eating their dinner and discussing her senseless story. It was clear what had likely gone through the madwoman's head. About three weeks earlier, Major Kappler had threatened Commander Foa, president of the Jewish community, and Doctor Almansi, head of the Union,[4] with the taking of 200 Jewish hostages. The numbers were the same, which explained her confusion. Poor people always learn things after everyone else and always indirectly, but the little that they do get to know, they always believe to be pure gold. By now, the threat of the 200 hostages had been

---

*4. Union of Italian Jewish Communities.

averted. The Germans may be *rashanim*,[5] but they are men of honor.

Contrary to general opinion, Jews are not distrustful by nature. Or to put it more clearly, they are distrustful in the same degree that they are perceptive about small matters, but credulous and disastrously ingenuous when it comes to large ones. In regard to the Germans, they were ingenuous, almost ostentatiously so. There are several possible reasons for this. Convinced by centuries of experience that it is their fate to be treated like dogs, Jews have a desperate need for human sympathy; and to solicit it, they offer it. To trust people, to rely on them, to believe in their promises, is precisely such a proof of sympathy. Will they behave this way with the Germans? Yes, unfortunately. With the Germans there would also come into play the classic Jewish attitude toward authority. Even before the first fall of Jerusalem, authority has exercised absolute, arbitrary, and inscrutable power of life and death over Jews. This has operated in such a way that both in their conscious and unconscious minds authority has assumed the form of an exclusive, jealous, and omnipotent God. To distrust His promises, whether good or bad, is to fall into sin for which sooner or later one will have to pay, even if that sin remains unexpressed, and is only an intention, or a mumbled complaint. And finally, the fundamental idea of Judaism is justice. The mission of the Jews was to bring this idea to Eastern civilization. Renan makes this expressly the theme of his interpretation of the entire history of Israel, including the great eschatological statements, in-

---

5. Evildoers.

cluding the Messianic wait, and the promise that on that Day of the Lord, tomorrow or who knows when, He will light His dawn at the height of the millennia precisely to bring back the reign of justice upon this earth.

For these reasons, Rome's Jews had a certain kind of faith in the Germans, even—we should say *particularly*—after all that happened on September 26. They felt as if they had been inoculated against further persecutions. Any such would have been an injustice, and their natures would not allow them to believe in that possibility. To show fear would have meant to antagonize the Germans—to reveal their antipathy to them. And finally it would have been a sin against Authority. So, on that evening, the Jews laughed at crazy Celeste's message.

(We beg forgiveness for this digression, and for any others in which we might indulge, but in order to understand the full horror of the drama which we seek to reconstruct, it is necessary to know the people involved a little better.)

In fact, on the evening of the 26th of September, 1943, the presidents of the Roman Jewish community and of the Union of the Italian Communities had been summoned—through Doctor Cappa, a police official—to a 6 P.M. meeting at the German Embassy. They were received with frightening courtesy and "politesse" by SS Major Herbert Kappler, who made them comfortable and spoke to them for a few minutes about this and that in conversational tones. Then he went to the heart of the matter. Roman Jews were doubly guilty, as Italians (but less than two months later a German-Fascist decree, sponsored by

Rahn, Mussolini, and Pavolini, will no longer recognize Italian Jews as citizens of Italy, and what then Major Kappler?), for their betrayal of Germany, and as Jews because they belong to a race eternally inimical to Germany. Therefore, the government of the Reich was levying a tribute of 50 kilograms of gold, to be produced before 11 A.M. of the following Tuesday, the 28th. Nonfulfillment would result in the roundup and deportation to Germany of two hundred Jews. Essentially, a little less than a day and a half to find 50 kilograms of gold.

Responding to the difficulties which the two Jewish representatives pointed out in opposition to the plan, the Major countered with a concession; he would furnish motor vehicles and men for searching out the gold. The two *Herren* would not accept? That's all right. It's as if it were never said. But in the same generous vein, he would extend the time for an additional hour. They asked him what the value of gold was in lire. Kappler understood the implications. "The German Reich," he answered, "has no need of lire. And if ever it should need them," he smiled, "it can always print them." Then he considered it appropriate to complete his presentation by announcing that in dealing with him there was no possibility for recalcitrance. Otherwise, he would take personal responsibility for the roundup. He had done so in several similar circumstances and had always succeeded very well at that type of operation. With which remark the subject appeared to be closed and the meeting was concluded.

Italian police headquarters, which was immediately informed of the exaction, did not respond. There were repeated messages, visits, telephone calls. Silence, to use a cruel allusion, was more than ever golden. So the same evening and the next morning the most influential members of the community, along with those known to be discreet, adept in business, and well-to-do, were gathered together. Disconsolate and distressed, they discussed the thing and declared it not doable. But the most forceful of them prevailed, and the collection of gold began. Word had already run through the Jewish community. Nevertheless, the offerings came very slowly at first, with a kind of uncertainty. It was during this period that the Vatican announced officially that it was putting 15 kilograms of gold at the disposition of the Jewish community to make up any eventual shortfall.

Meanwhile things had begun to improve. By then, all of Rome had learned of the German outrage and had been moved by it. Warily, as if fearing a refusal, as if intimidated to be coming to offer gold to the wealthy Jews, several "Aryans" appeared. They entered the room adjacent to the synagogue uncertainly, not knowing whether they ought to remove their hats or keep their heads covered as, all of them knew, Jewish ritual required. Almost humbly, they asked if they too could . . . if it would be acceptable. . . . Unfortunately, they did not leave their names. One would have liked to have a record of them for those moments when we lose faith in our fellow beings. Which brings to mind a fitting phrase that George Eliot used, "The milk of human kindness."

The collection station was set up in one of the Jewish community offices. The police, whose deaf ear finally began hearing, assigned men to keep order and stand guard. The flow, in fact, had begun to be remarkable. At the table sat a trusted member of the community. Next to him, a goldsmith assayed the offerings, and another weighed them. At the very first, word had been sent out that cash contributions were not acceptable. This would have slowed the flow of metal. Gold objects often represent cherished memories, which tend to become even more memorable, and more cherished, at the moment of parting from them. Moreover, during periods of war and disasters, gold has proved itself the best and most portable asset for dire emergencies. Cash, on the other hand, would have come in plentifully and quickly. It would, however, have created a problem, not least, the risk of locating that much gold on the black market. But the metal already was beginning to pile up, and so many people had come offering gold for sale, that they even began to accept cash and to buy gold on the basis of varying prices. The woman at the newsstand on the Ponte Garibaldi helped greatly with these purchases.

By 11 A.M. Tuesday morning the full amount had been gathered, with even a surplus of more than two million in cash, which was put aside in the community safe. The collection room was closed and locked. Outside the door, along with police agents, sat the goldsmiths and several community representatives. A cultured and witty German opera-lover might perhaps have joked about these Fafners[6] guarding their treasure. Instead, as their wives had brought these good people food, far from vomiting flames, they ate their meal in peace. Their consciences were clear. There

---

*6. Dragon who guards the Rhine gold in Wagner's ring cycle.

had been moments of anxiety, feverish clock-watching, but all things considered, their work had gone well.

A call was put in to the German ambassador in order to obtain an extension of a few hours. It was a precaution in view of the prompt attainment of their goal, to forestall any increase in the demand. The blessed naiveté of the shrewd! As if the Germans wouldn't have had spies. Nevertheless, they obtained an extension until 6 P.M., at which hour three automobiles set off from Lungotevere Sanzio[7] with the gold, the two presidents, the two goldsmiths, and a police escort, again led by Doctor Cappa, in the direction of Villa Wolkonski.[8]

Let alone sink to the formality of receiving them and of "collecting" all that gold, Kappler didn't even deign to appear. He had a secretary tell them in the antechamber that the ransom would have to be deposited on via Tasso.[9] This is perhaps the first appearance of via Tasso in the criminally black chronicle of the German occupation. The convoy leaves via Wolkonski, turns the corner, and reaches the infamous street.

On via Tasso the Jews found themselves before a certain Captain Schultz,[10] certainly one far more cruel than the Schultz of our old Latin grammars. The man was assisted by a goldsmith and a weigher, both German. The gold had been packed into ten of those cardboard containers, the size of large file boxes used in offices to store correspon-

---

*7. Still the address of Jewish community offices.
*8. German Embassy.
*9. Gestapo Headquarters.
*10. Schutz in the Jewish community's report and others.

dence. To repeat, there were ten—and each contained five kilograms of metal. To weigh and examine them must have been the easiest thing in the world to do.

But 8 P.M. came and went and neither the presidents nor the goldsmiths had yet returned to their residences. The tick-tock of the clocks in the silence of those homes were to their families like the gnawing of anxiety, measuring out minute by minute ever more grievous conjectures. An absurd trilling of the telephone. But the men weren't calling. Their friends were, those who had worked most assiduously with them to collect the gold, and who now hung up their phones with words meant to sound confident, and yet sounded mournful.

Finally the four men returned, filled with that mixture of relief and exhaustion that completely takes over one's being after an enormous strain. The feeling was a little like that of someone who returns from having accompanied a loved one to the cemetery along a long road in inclement weather, when one was already exhausted by bedside vigils and anxiety. You eat something, throw yourself in bed, try not to think of it any more.

What had happened? They themselves didn't understand it clearly. At the end of a first inspection, the German, in a tone that allowed no challenge, had claimed that there were only nine boxes. How could anyone think that the Jews would have tried to cheat the Reich? There's always enough iron to retemper Brennus's sword.[11] Long,

---

*11. After a seven-month siege of Rome in 391 B.C., Brennus, chief of the invading Celts, demanded 1,000 pounds of gold to

quibbling, and dramatic discussions followed. Captain Schultz refused any recounting. Until finally, the counting and weighing were repeated, almost arrogantly, and there were undeniably ten boxes of correct weight, with even a few grams in excess. Nevertheless, Captain Schultz had refused to give them a receipt.

Why? It was thought that the Germans did not want to leave behind any documentation of the outrage. But they have left and will leave plenty of other kinds of documentation; in pits, in places of slaughter, in establishments blown up by mines, in their plundering. With their every step they've left them and are leaving them, and they are such that they are etched into Europe's surface and will remain so for decades to come. Oh, perhaps no one would dare put a *personal* signature under such a document? The Moscow Accords on the responsibilities and the punishments of war crimes would not be stipulated until long afterwards, but to the criminal mind there's always a sense of the inevitability of punishment. More probably, the explanation of the refusal can be sought in the events that followed, considering the likelihood that to the Germans, creators of paper-scrapping notions, any receipt or contract would constitute a bond or obligation.

Did Captain Schultz know by then what preparations were being made for the following day? There's no doubt that Major Kappler of the SS knew of them, because it was

---

leave the city in peace. The money was raised with difficulty, and at the weighing the Romans accused the Celts of using false weights, whereupon Brennus threw his own sword onto the scales, calling out, "*Vae victus*," Woe to the defeated.

an SS squad which appeared at the community offices the following morning, the 29th of September, and carted off archives, documents, registers, everything they could find, including of course, the two million in cash left over from the collection of the gold. Except for that, their visit wasn't very profitable. The Temple's furnishings and its most precious objects had already been removed to safety. Which was, we believe, one of the very few precautions taken by the Jews.

It would be interesting to know more about the strange figure who appears at the offices of the Jewish community on October 11. He too is escorted by SS troops and appears to be just another German officer, but with an extra dose of arrogance that comes from having a privileged and, regrettably, well-known "specialty." Like the others, from head to toe he is all uniform—that close-fitting fastidiously elegant, abstract, and implacable uniform which, airtight as a zipper, locks in the wearer's body and, above all, his mind. It is the word *verboten* translated into uniform; access forbidden to the man and to the personal experiences he has lived through, to his past, and truest *uniqueness* as a human being on this earth; access forbidden to the sight of anything but his *present*, stern, programmed, unyielding.

While his men commence ransacking the libraries of the rabbinical college and the Jewish community, the officer, with hands as cautious and sensitive as those of the finest needlewoman, skims, touches, caresses papyri and incunabula, leafs through manuscripts and rare editions, peruses parchments and palimpsests. The varying degrees of caution in his touch, the heedfulness of his gestures, are quickly adapted to the importance of each work. Those texts were, for the most part, written in exotic alphabets. But when the officer opens to a page, as happens to certain particularly gifted readers, who can instantly find desired and meaningful passages, his gaze is riveted, his eyes become bright. In those aristocratic hands, the books, as though subjected to the cruel and bloodless torture of an exquisite sadism, revealed everything. Later, it became known that the SS officer was a distinguished scholar of paleography and Semitic philology.

The library of the rabbinical college of Rome and, even more so, the Jewish community library contained extraordinary collections and rare editions, some of them unique. Neither a complete study of the library's holdings nor a catalogue had yet been prepared. Perhaps they would have revealed other treasures. What we do know is that there were a great many documents and chronicles in manuscript and print, dealing with the diaspora of the Mediterranean basin, as well as primary sources relating to the entire history and origins of the Roman Jews, the closest and most direct descendants of ancient Judaism. Fresh descriptions, unknown views of Caesar's Rome, of its emperors and popes were hiding in those writings. And generations who indeed seem to have passed on this earth like autumn leaves lay waiting deep in those pages for someone to bid them to speak.

A quick jerk of the zipper and the uniform has closed off the scholar of Semitic philology, who once more has become an SS officer. He issues an order. Anyone who touches, hides, or removes so much as a single volume will be shot in accordance with German military law.[12] He leaves. His heels click down the stairs. Shortly thereafter, three large freight cars arrive on the tracks of the Black Tram line. The SS load the two libraries onto them. The cars leave. Books, manuscripts, codices, parchments are on their way to Munich.

Who knows if it will be these very same freight cars which will shortly be called upon to carry another, a very different, living, cargo to Germany? There was time enough to get there and back—five days. And again, we ask ourselves this one last time, as if the question could still sound the alarm to those it concerns—with such persistent provocations, why not think of fleeing to safety? Well, the theft of the books wasn't a provocation to the ghetto Jews, who knew little about books. On the other hand, it was precisely they, those of the *Piazza Giudìa,* who should have been most alert to the menace, as they were destined to become the prime booty of the roundup. But would they have even heeded an alarm? They were phlegmatic and attached to their immediate surroundings. The wandering Jew is tired by now, he has walked too much and can't go on. The exertion of the many exiles, flights, and deportations, of the many roads traversed by ancestors for century after century, has resulted in damage to the sons' muscles. Their legs refuse to keep on dragging their flat feet. And

---

12. Naturally, the community representatives sent an appeal to the Ministry of the Interior and another to the Ministry of National Culture, both of which met the same fate as the appeal sent to the police several days earlier.

then there was, without a doubt, there was a fifth column, whose goal it was to "disseminate reassurance." For example, several Jews had been arrested on October 8. Many others became frightened that this might have been the beginning of individual persecutions. Immediately, in reply, the reassuring news was circulated (and responsible members of the community doubtlessly with good intentions, helped circulate it) that those who'd been arrested were exceptional cases, people previously known for their anti-Fascist activities. They had been targeted not for their race, but for their actions. The Germans continued to behave discreetly, almost humanely. With their overwhelming power, with their absolute authority, *they could have done many worse things.* And instead . . . No, there was no special reason not to trust them, or to take the worst possible view of things.

So the Jews were sleeping in their beds around midnight on Friday, October 15, when the streets began resounding with gunfire and explosions. Beginning on July 25, when Badoglio had instituted the curfew, and more frequently after September 8, almost every night they'd hear shots in the streets and tell themselves it was aimed at people out past the curfew without permits. But those shots were generally discreet, like a clock striking the hour; rarely were they heard so close by and never so persistently. These, on the other hand, intensify, sound ever closer together, overlap, and become a veritable barrage. And would that they were only shots, but a more ominous sound is mixed among them. Explosions that start out crisply then spread almost in waves, and flare deep craters in the darkness. *Baruch dajan emed.*[13] It sounds like the middle of a battle. There are some who wake and sit up in bed. But there's no one who still remembers the warning they'd received at nightfall in the piazza in Trastevere.

The courageous go to their windows. Bullets and shards whistle and whine a few inches from their shutters and penetrate the ancient plaster facades. Through the shutters, through the clammy drizzle, between flashes of gunfire and the glare of explosives, they see squads of soldiers in the street shooting into the air and throwing grenades at the sidewalks. By their helmets they would guess they're Germans, but they'd only taken a brief glimpse. It's not safe to stay at the window. Now the *jorbetin*[14] have begun screaming and yelling as well— shattering, furious, taunting incomprehensible words and shouts. What do they want? Who are they after? Where are they going?

In the houses, everyone is out of bed by now. Neighbors gather to try to keep their spirits up but only succeed in frightening each other. Children scream. What can you say to silence children when you don't know what to say to yourself? Be good now. They're on their way to Monte Savello. To Piazza Cairoli. You'll see, it'll be over in a few minutes. But it isn't over at all. They seem to be going away, but then here they are again, and all the while the

---

13. Blessed be the Judge of Truth. (*Transliterated into English, the phrase would read *Baruch dayan emet*. It is generally translated as Blessed be the one true Judge—and is associated with facing death.)

14. Soldiers.

shooting has never stopped. If only they did something, smashed through a door, a gate, or into a store—at least you'd understand why. But no, all they do is shoot and shout. It's like a toothache—there's no knowing how long it will last, how much worse it can get. This not understanding is the worst of their anxieties. A woman who gave birth a few hours earlier can no longer stand the strain, and leaping from her bed, grabs her newborn and rushes into a neighbor's dining room, where she faints. Women revive her: cognac, hot-water bottles—this at least is part of everyday life, of misfortunes they can alleviate. But down in the street, the shooting and shouting has been going on—two hours, three hours, more than three hours.

Every year at the Passover meal—*let whoever is hungry come and eat*—one sets aside half a piece of matzoh. A belief, handed down from who knows what ancient times, perhaps from when the Jews were still farmers, has it that a piece of that unleavened bread, thrown from the window, will calm hurricanes, tempests, and hailstorms which destroy crops, ruin grapevines and olives, and threaten famine, perhaps death. Who knows whether it occurred to anyone that night to take the matzoh left over from the previous Passover—the last time they had commemorated the flight from Egypt and liberation from the Pharaohs—and of throwing it into that inferno in the streets. The grain had been harvested, the vines gleaned, but there was another crop that needed to be saved, the progeny of Israel, which the Patriarchs had been promised would be as numerous as sands of the sea. Yet had the harmless matzoh fallen from a window, the Germans would have aimed their rifles and machine guns, hurled their grenades at that window.

Only they knew the reason for that hell. And perhaps the real reason was precisely that there was no reason—a gratuitous hell, so that it would be more mysterious and therefore more frightening. At the time people assumed it was meant to be insulting, a spiteful anti-Semitic act. Later, with logic and hindsight, it was thought that the Germans deliberately frightened the Ghetto residents—compelled them to shut themselves in their homes, so that in case something of the next day's plans had leaked out they could still all be taken.

Toward four o'clock in the morning the shooting subsided. It was cold, the dampness of the rainy night penetrated the walls. Having been roused in the middle of the night, everyone was in nightclothes and slippers, with only a shawl or coat over their shoulders. Perhaps their empty beds would still have a little warmth. Tired, with that sense of hollowness and dryness that strong emotion leaves behind the eye sockets, with aching bones and chattering teeth, people returned to their own homes and their beds. In two hours it would be daylight—they would finally know something. But then again, when you really think about it, "*nothing had happened.*"

It appears that a woman named Letizia, known to the neighborhood as Goggle-eyed Letizia, sounded the first alarm. She's a large, elderly, fleshy-featured spinster with staring eyes and thick protruding lips that set a rigid, meaningless grin on her face. The voice she emits is distracted, irritated, and detached from her words. Toward 5 A.M. she was heard shouting, "Oh God, *i mammoni.*"

Mammoni in Roman Jewish slang means cops, guards, police. In fact, it was the Germans, who, with the heavy, cadenced steps (we know people for whom that step has remained the symbol, the terrifying audio equivalent, of the German horrors) had begun to barricade streets and houses of the Ghetto. The owner of a small café near the Portico di Ottavia—a non-Jew, who, from the favorable position of his shop was able to witness events as they unfolded around him—had just arrived there from his home in Testaccio. Passing through Monte Sabello and the Portico, he hadn't noticed anything out of the ordinary. (Would there have been time to save oneself after the gunfire in the streets? Or was the quarter already surrounded?) He says that he himself first heard the rhythmic steps toward 5:30 (it hasn't been possible to get the witnesses to agree on the exact time: that disastrous moment must have been dreadfully elastic, subject only to psychological measure). He hadn't yet opened his shop. He was just pressurizing the espresso machine. He opened a shutter partway and watched.

He watched two columns of German soldiers coming along the sidewalks. He figured there were about a hundred of them. Officers standing in the middle of the street were stationing armed guards at every intersection. A few passersby stopped to watch. The Germans paid them no heed. It was only much later that they seized anyone carrying packages or suitcases, indications of attempted flight.

We will return to the story of the Ghetto because it was at the epicenter of the roundup. But there were other places in the city where the work had been begun several hours earlier. There's the fact, for example, that Sternberg Monteldi, a lawyer from Trieste, had been arrested at 11 o'clock the night before at the Hotel Vittoria where he and his wife were staying. This is the point at which the questions about the criteria and the procedures that governed the roundup come to the fore. The lawyer and his wife had Swiss passports, therefore their names did not appear on any register of the Roman population. They had not filled out any racial declarations, therefore were not considered Jews. How did their names get to the SS? As to the procedures employed, it is known that in this case the arrest was made in the harshest way. The couple was forced to get dressed in the presence of the soldiers, who kept their guns trained on them.

This premature beginning could have severely jeopardized the Germans' plans. It would have been enough had the news spread, as it did the following morning the instant the roundup began in earnest, racing through the entire city so that friends and even police officers were able to warn people, at least those they could reach by telephone.

Had such an alarm come the previous evening, it would have emptied at least half the Jewish households. Instead, although the Sternbergs' arrest took place in a hotel, it remained unknown. The gossip of the domestic staff and the night clerk was not sufficient for it to leak out. As far as is known, not even the police department got wind of it. So the next morning the Germans found it possible to do their work methodically, according to plan and with the fullest measure of success.

Now we enter a house on via S. Ambrogio in the Ghetto. We'll be able to watch the entire raid from here. Toward 5 A.M. (a psychologically meaningful time, we repeat) Signora Laurina S. hears herself called from the street.

It's her niece shouting, "Auntie, auntie, come down! The Germans are taking everyone away."

A few minutes before, on leaving her house on via della Reginella, this girl had seen an entire family with six children, the oldest of which was ten, being taken away. Signora S. looks out the window. She sees two Germans, one on each side of the doorway, armed with rifles or machine guns (she can't tell which). Here, one wonders how the niece could have shouted such explicit words in the presence of the Germans. The street was extremely narrow, just an alley. And we must explain again that for the most part the Germans did not round up people on the street. Out of doors they took only those poor souls who took no precautions to keep from being taken. Nor is it necessary to think that the tragedy was enacted in an atmosphere of muted and astonished solemnity. People went on talking among themselves, shouting out news, suggestions, as they do in ordinary life. Destiny performed its serious work without troubling itself with ceremony, without concern for the trivia of style. Tragedy entered the stream of life and blended into it with such terrifying naturalness that from the first there was no room for anything, not even astonishment.

At first Signora S. assumed, as everyone else did, that the Germans had come to take the men for "labor duty." This idea, probably deliberately disseminated, was the ruination of many families, who never thought of sheltering old people, women, and children. Therefore, presuming the immunity of women, Signora S. plucks up her courage, dresses as best she can, takes her ration cards and shopping bag, then goes downstairs to try to find out what's going on. A few days earlier she had fallen and is now dragging one leg in a cast.

When she gets outside, she approaches the German sentries and offers them cigarettes, which they accept. One of them could be about twenty-five years old, the other seems to be about forty. Just as in all books like *My Prisons*[15] there's almost always a good jailer, so in this raid there will be kindhearted SS men. These two, for example. The tale that formed about them subsequently in the Ghetto has it that they were Austrian.

"Taking away all the Jews," the older of the two answers the woman. She slaps her hand against her plaster cast.

"But I have a broken leg—going with my family—hospital."

"Ja, ja," the Austrian nods and gestures with his hand that she can slip away. But while she waits for her family, Signora S. decides to take advantage of her friendship with the two soldiers and save some neighbors. Now it is she who calls up from the street.

"Sterina, Sterina."

"What's the matter?" the woman answers from her window.

"Get out. They're taking everyone."

"In a minute. I'll dress the baby and be right down."

Unfortunately dressing the baby was fatal. Signora Sterina, her baby, and entire family were taken.

---

*15. *Le mie prigioni* is a 19th-century memoir by the Italian, Silvio Pellico, of his years in an Austrian prison. It is known for its remarkably gentle tone.

October 16, 1943

Lamentations and shouts sound from via Portico di Ottavia. Signora S. peers around the corner of via Sant' Ambrogio and the Portico. It's really true that they are taking everyone, every single one, worse than anyone could have imagined. The captured families are straggling single-file down the middle of the street. SS troopers at the head and the tail of each little band are guarding them, keeping them more or less in line, prodding them on with the butts of their machine guns although no one is resisting with anything more than tears, moans, cries for mercy, confused questions. More than even suffering, the faces and bearings of these Jews are already marked with resignation. It's as if that heinous, unexpected, sudden roundup no longer astonishes them. Something in them recalls their unknown forefathers, who had walked at the same pace, driven on by oppressors like these, toward deportation, slavery, torture, and the stake. The mothers, or sometimes fathers, are carrying the smallest children in their arms, holding the older ones by the hand. The children search their parents' eyes for reassurance, comfort the latter can no longer give, and this is even more devastating than having to say, "there isn't any" to a child asking for bread. On the other hand, it is just a question of time. If they aren't killed first, they'll come to that moment too. Some of them kiss their children, a kiss that they try to hide from the Germans, a last kiss surrounded by the streets, the houses, the sites that witnessed their birth, and the first smiles of their lives. And there are fathers who keep their hands on their child's head in the very same manner with which, on holy days, they had bestowed the *Birchad Cho-*

anim.[16] "May the Lord bless you and keep you . . ."—the blessing that invokes and promises peace to the children of Israel.

Signora S. also saw old Aunt Chele, who's about eighty years old and half out of her mind, in the line. She was swept along among the others, almost skipping a little, without understanding what was happening to her, and was responding to the stares of people around her with greetings and inane, even fatuous smiles. But she jumped with fright and began murmuring fragments of prayers when the Germans began shouting again. They were shouting for no good reason, probably only to maintain an air of terror and a sense of their authority, so that they wouldn't run into any snags and would get the whole thing done quickly. Another old woman, eighty-five years old, deaf and sick goes by. A paralytic carried aloft in his chair goes by. A woman with a nursing child in her arms opens her blouse and takes out a breast and presses it to demonstrate to a soldier that there is no longer any milk for her child. But he pokes his machine gun into her side to get her to walk. Another woman seizes the hand of a German and kisses it, weeping, to soften his heart, to ask him for who knows what trivial favor, perhaps only because she is grateful, from the depths of her humiliation, that he hasn't treated her worse. A blow and a shout are her answer. At the sides of the street, stunned passersby, unable to help, stand rigidly and watch. Eventually, the Germans no longer want to have these spectators around and menacingly order them to get moving.

---

16. Priestly blessing.

A young man leaves the line—he has obtained permission to get some coffee under the surveillance of an SS man, who, however, will not agree "to keep him company." He sips it noisily, the small cup trembles in his hands and his legs wobble. He turns his dazed eyes toward the small tables where he used to sit and play cards on evenings that still had a tomorrow. With a kind of embarrassed, weary smile, he asks the café owner, "What are they going to do with us?"

These poor pathetic words are among the few left to us by those in the process of departing. In them we hear the voice of a human being restored for a moment to life, living with us, when he is no longer a part of our lives and has already entered into that new, terrible, dark, existence. And they tell us as well what was going through the minds of those poor, unfortunate souls in the first moments—the hopeless hope that they had misunderstood what was happening to them.

The lines were being directed toward the ugly little Museum of Antiquity and Fine Arts, which rises at the summit of Portico di Ottavia in front of via Catalan, between the church of Sant' Angelo and the Teatro di Marcello. At the foot of the museum building, there's a small excavated area, several meters below street level, that's cluttered with ruins. The Jews were gathered together in this pit and arranged in lines to await the return of three or four trucks, which were shuttling back and forth between the Ghetto and the site that had been set up as the first staging area. These trucks were covered by tarpaulins (it was still drizzling). The tarpaulins were dark, some say they were actually black—these same people say the trucks were black as well. It's more likely that all that blackness was perceived by distraught, sorrow-filled eyes. In reality the trucks must have been painted in the murky, depressing enough mud-and-lead color, which is the standard finish of German military vehicles. Nazis love creating productions, theatricality, dark, dread-filled Nibelungian solemnity. But here the production was in the circumstances themselves. And unnecessary too, because everything unfolded with extreme ease, without their having to induce success with any particular staging or special effects.

The trucks' right sideboards were lowered and the loading began. The sick, the disabled, and balky were urged on by insults, shouts, shoves, and blows from gun stocks. The paralyzed man in his chair was literally flung into the truck like a discarded piece of furniture onto a moving van. As to children snatched from their mothers' arms, they were subject to the treatment packages undergo when postal workers load their vans. And the trucks would leave again, no one knew for where, but the regularity of the return of the same ones led to the belief that they weren't going too far away. And perhaps this might have sparked some hope among the victims. They're not sending us out of Rome. They're keeping us here to work.

We resume following Signora S. Her tale, doubtlessly repeated many times in the past few months, will certainly have been somewhat reconstructed—in the order of facts and sequence of events, which perhaps they did not have in real life. But the people she refers to—those it's been possible to question—confirm the truth of the events and the precision of the details.

Having arrived with her family at Largo Argentina, that is, having by now crossed the Red Sea, Signora S. hears about a relative who, for fear of those guards posted at the door, had remained upstairs. (A frequent and unfortunate situation; because of that fear, many were unwilling to leave their apartments and thus were captured there.) In spite of her family's protests, Signora S. decides to go back and rescue the relative if she can get there in time. This might seem an excess of bravado, too much of a good thing. Nevertheless there are people whom extreme circumstances endow with exuberant vitality which in turn creates a belief in their own invulnerability. It's the same with those nurses who make their rounds during epidemics with a carefree, almost irritating, disdain for prophylaxis, and nevertheless are precisely the ones who get away with it, as if disease had no power over them.

The two "Austrians" are still at the door. Just a glance is enough to reassure the signora that their tacit pact is still in effect. She calls up to the relative from the stairwell.

"*Resciud,*[17] Enrico."

But just at that moment seven German soldiers arrive. They've heard her call and no matter that they didn't understand it, their leader decides to give Signora S. a slap that sends her sprawling across the doorway. Then, with incomprehensible German words, and too easily understood threats with the butt of his machine gun, he prods

---

17. "Get away."

her to get up unaided. Two soldiers place themselves in front of her, three behind her, and force her up the stairs. On the landing, the doors of three apartments are bolted shut (one is the now-deserted S. family apartment).

The dramatic intensity and complexity of the actions that are about to take place on this landing might cause one to visualize an appropriate, one might even say an Aeschylean, setting. But that would not accord with reality. This is a tiny area, not even two square meters, which interrupts a spiral staircase made up of filthy stone steps encrusted with old refuse, set between two oppressive walls. This is a hovel—even if we didn't know it was destined to suffering, and how much suffering it underwent!—in which poverty and misery have a hostile, almost sinister desolation. Every one of life's odors has permeated its walls, wood and iron, even, one might almost say, the panes of its tiny windows. Such, or very like it, were the buildings which housed the majority of the most terrible enemies of the Great German Reich.

The Germans consulted a typed list. Unfortunately, two of the doors bore the silly affectation of a nameplate on the knocker. And the names corresponded to those on the list. The Germans knocked on them, then, not receiving any response, broke the doors down.

Behind them, stony and stiff as if posing for the most frighteningly surrealistic of family portraits, their residents stood in terrified attention—their eyes as though hypnotized and their hearts in their mouths. The alarm had been sounded almost an hour before, but in their agitation of conferring about fleeing, salvaging a few possessions, in the tumult of ineffective and contradictory decisions, almost none of them had found time to get dressed. Most were still in nightclothes or, at best, had put on an old coat or a threadbare jacket.

The squad leader goes up to them. He has a kind of typewritten card in his hand from which he reads in German. All they understand is his peremptory, menacing tone. The women and children burst into tears. Signora S. has had time to notice that her name is not on the list. This gives her courage. As if to avenge herself for the slap, she snatches the card from the German's hands. The text is bilingual. And it is she who reads it in a loud voice to her neighbors.

1. You, your family, and other Jews in your household are being moved.
2. You must take with you:
   a) food for at least eight days
   b) ration cards
   c) identification cards
   d) drinking glasses.
3. You may take with you:
   a) a small suitcase with personal effects and belongings, linen, blankets, etc.
   b) money and jewelry.
4. Lock your apartment up—also the house. Take along the key.
5. The sick, even those gravely ill, cannot under any circumstances remain behind. There are hospitals in the camp.
6. Your family must be ready to leave twenty minutes after receipt of this card.

Twenty minutes; no time even to complain. Much less time enough to get things together. The good glasses—it'll be better to leave them at home. And suitcases, where are we going to get one for everybody? The children will need one for themselves. Never mind that. Just be sure the Germans don't see where the *manhòd*[18] is hidden. There's no jewelry around any more. It's all with a *nharel*.[19] The crucial words have to be spoken in Hebrew of the only kind they know, in that jargon that sounds like thieves' slang, and has always created the suspicion that Jews were involved in a conspiracy. But how else to talk with those two soldiers in the house watching their preparations? The children cling to their mothers' skirts but are not allowed to hold on. Some of them get slapped across the face. Jews are quick to use their hands in dealing with their children.

The soldiers still out on the landing approach Signora S. and ask her if she is related to those families. No, she is not related. If she is a *Juda*. No, she isn't a *Juda*. Give them proof. The Signora takes out her key, opens her apartment door to show that is her home, that she doesn't live with the others, that she has nothing in common with them. They force her into the apartment and order her to shut the door. The twenty minutes allowed to her neighbors have almost expired. As the Germans hurry them on, the cries and pleas start again. In the confusion of making their preparations they've almost forgotten that these are preparations for being taken from their homes. Signora S. can no longer stand it. She goes out onto the landing. The

18. Money.
19. Catholic.

Germans are about to shove her back in, but she turns and points to her leg in the cast. She has to go to the hospital. One of them indicates that she is free, that she'd better get out of there quickly.

Just at that moment, seeing her start down the staircase, four children rush from the two apartments and clutch her arms and her dress. "Help us, Laurina! Laurina, save us." One of the four is the then little twelve-year-old Esther P. She explains that she came to sleep over at her aunt's that night because very early this morning she had to get on the ration line for vegetables and she'd been afraid of going out alone in the dark. The moment she and her aunt were out in the street, they saw Germans stationed at every street corner. Immediately they went back home. Auntie thought (and so did she) that the Germans had come to take the men, and Auntie wanted to give her husband some money so that he could escape. Had they continued going down the street, at least the two of them would have been saved. Instead they were trapped because shortly thereafter the seven Germans had come up. When she realized that she too was being taken away, the child's biggest fear was that her father would be furious at her for not coming right home. Even Auntie, rushing between the wardrobe and the chest of drawers, packing things, was telling her, "Get out of here, go back home or your father will give me what-for later."

This idea of a scolding and even more of a "later" tells us many things. They went on thinking of an "afterwards" as though their earlier lives would continue on as before. (And yet the card had put it clearly.) Without a doubt there were people who were more aware, who immediately understood what was happening. But to most of those who lived around the Piazza Giudìa, it was as if they had taken a relative to a doctor who makes a diagnosis that leaves no hope. For a while they repeat the name of the illness, they make observations about it, almost getting to feel familiar with it, as if it were the name of one of the many illnesses that they already know, that have already passed through the household. Only much later, do they understand what the name implies, what the name holds for them.

Signora S. clasped the children to her, said that they were hers. The Germans didn't challenge her. As soon as she and the children were far enough down the street, the children slipped away from her. Signora S. took a few more steps and then fainted. Some "Aryans" came to her rescue and carried her to the café at Ponte Garibaldi.

It may seem strange that this woman who thrust herself so fearlessly into the heart of that roundup, almost without missing any opportunity to jeopardize her own safety, wasn't recognized to be Jewish and taken away herself. Just as it also seems strange that the Germans had so readily conceded the four children to her. It's already been said that above all they operated on the basis of their lists. And some may be tempted to add that Germans usually lack intelligence and imagination. They follow orders without any input of their own.

To which, however, one could reply that, on the other hand, cruelty is always shrewd in its way, or at least mistrustful and alert. All things considered, the impression remains that the SS, already inured to this type of operation, had acted that morning with a kind of professional rigor, with a consciousness of their trade, rather than from the stimulus of specific fury. The brutality that they demonstrated, one could say, was part of their technique and only

53

exceptionally became an act of individual sadism. Driven by motor power, the fly wheel, which is itself forced by the workings of the gears, expends all its energy in crushing the unlucky creature caught in it, but will not shift even a millimeter to find itself a victim. For that reason, the roundup that morning did not, generally speaking, turn into a hunt for Jews. For example, the famous weekly distributions of cigarettes were, for once, really providential. Many men escaped because they were on line at the tobacconists, and not one German soldier bothered to go looking for them there. Fate was holding some of them aside for the Ardeatine Caves. (Many were rounded up or captured later, mostly after February 1944, by the same Germans, or still later by the Fascists. Most of them ended up in northern Italian concentration camps—Modena and Verona—until later in April when they were deported to Germany.) In essence, the SS acted primarily *as if* their responsibility was to furnish their superiors a certain—and without doubt—a very considerable number of Jews. And seeing that goal was easy to reach, they didn't trouble themselves to put too fine a point on it, or to get overzealous in the attempt.

But there are examples to the contrary, which demonstrate that the presumed rule was subject to so many exceptions that it ended up deceiving anyone who believed it, becoming a trap for those who relied on it. Our mistake is to want to find a rule in the most terrifying arbitrariness. A certain woman named N. had taken refuge in the café. Suddenly she heard louder and more excited voices approaching in the street. A young man, who later described himself as an Italian journalist, was arguing in German with an SS man to try to get a pregnant woman off the line already headed toward a truck. Signora N. recognizes the woman as her own sister, whose fate she hadn't known. She can't hide a gesture of shocked sorrow. A German notices it, infers the relationship, rushes at N. and takes her away with the little daughter standing at her side. Another woman thought of herself as saved; her husband, who had been poorly hidden in a water tank, had been taken. She and her four children, two of whom are sick with diphtheria and have a high fever, had fled and were already at the Ponte Garibaldi. She sees a truck laden with relatives pass and emits a shout. The Germans fly at her, seize her and her children. An "Aryan" intervenes and manages to save one of the little girls protesting that she is his. But the child starts crying that she wants to be with mamma and she too is taken.

We've spoken many times about the infamous lists. Even these were more arbitrary than one can imagine, with equally inexplicable inclusions and omissions. How they were compiled, and on what basis, no one has yet managed to understand. However, in the meantime, we can exclude the possibility that the names were taken from documents stolen from the community's records. Those were lists of contributors, while the German's list was made up mostly of families who had never made any contributions. Others say that the local Fascist groups had complete lists of "citizens of the Jewish race" living within the jurisdiction of the group. But these agencies had been subject to attacks by anti-Fascists after the 25th of July. Moreover, the omissions and additions on the German lists raise a doubt that those could have been the source. The same for police precincts, also possessed of information of that nature, which during the Fascist days were useful for the petty harassment of Jews (calling them to *audiendum verbum*,[20] searching for hidden radios, visiting to check on whether they had Aryan servants, and so on). Or perhaps the Germans had recourse to the Directory of Demography and Race at the Ministry of the Interior? But then one wonders, why, after July 25, with the racial campaign over, the ministry didn't think of disposing of those now superfluous registries and files. And if not after July 25, why not, at least after September 8, as other ministries did with other documents?

In September, the negligence of July becomes criminal responsibility. In the days before the roundup, the Germans had spent long hours at the offices of the rationing board, rummaging through files and making notes, on the pretext of an impending distribution of new food cards. Could the lists have come from there? But no one ever noticed any indication of race on a ration card, and the Germans would therefore have had to make a set of long and difficult comparisons with their own manuals of Jewish surnames. The writer of this account spent the morning of October 16 in the house of a neighbor. This woman let it slip that she had anticipated the roundup. Actually, an acquaintance of hers, employed at the Registry Office, had confided to her a few days earlier, that they were being worked to death preparing certain lists of Jews for the Germans. On returning to Rome the following July, we tried to reopen the discussion with her, but it was completely

---

*20. "Literally, "The word must be listened to." The term derives from the era when Jews were forced to listen to sermons in church. Here they were Fascist "sermons."

hopeless. The woman was utterly nonplussed, had no memory of having known anything, much less having said anything of the sort.

The weather, which had remained rainy and dark all morning, cleared briefly at about 11 A.M. A little sunshine glowed on the paving stones of the Portico di Ottavia, along which those poor feet had been dragging for hours, those so often derided flat feet, so tired and painful before beginning their journey. On by now distant Sabbaths, that ray of sunlight would pierce the windows of the synagogue and gild the organ pipes, which would reply to it in their most golden register. And that ray of light would pour down on the faithful in a harmony of jubilation, in a glow of holy joy. The children would sing, "*Holy, holy, holy, the Lord of hosts. All the earth is filled with His glory.*" Now, from the depths of the pit in which they stand awaiting deportation, these children raise only laments, laments not joined in chorus, which do not rise toward heaven like the smoke of sacrifice; and which heaven, dark and low once again, seems to reject and send falling back upon their shoulders. How many years will still have to pass before that lament becomes the canticle of children in the fiery furnace? Before the Lord of Hosts hears them, once again rapt in the celebration of His glory?

The roundup lasted until about 1 P.M. When it was over, there wasn't a soul to be seen on the streets of the Ghetto, the desolation of Jeremiah's Jerusalem was upon it, *quomodo sedet sola civitas.*[21] All of Rome was stunned. In

---

21. "How doth the city sit solitary (that was full of people)" is the first line of the Lamentations of Jeremiah. The Latin phrase also begins chapter 28 of Dante's *Vita Nuova*.

other neighborhoods the raids had followed the same pattern as in the Ghetto, but of course, their yields were mere trickles. The city had been divided into several sectors, with a truck assigned to each of them, which proceeded down the streets stopping at the front doors noted on the list. Early in the morning, when they found the doors still closed, the SS had the Italian police open them. Usually a noncommissioned officer would remain in the truck, while two enlisted men would go up to the apartments. If the apartment seemed middle-class or comfortable, the first thing the soldiers did was to find the telephone and pull out the wires. There's a story that in Prati, a worker, having noticed the momentary distraction of a soldier left on guard, jumped into the truck and sped off with its cargo, all of whom unexpectedly found themselves free. (However, I, personally, was never able to find any of these miraculous escapees.)

The SS who performed this roundup belonged to a special unit which, unknown to all the other German troops stationed in Rome, had arrived from the North the previous evening. They didn't know their way around the city and hadn't had time to reconnoiter the parts of it in which they were to work, so that, in fact, one of the units ordered to the Ghetto stopped on the via del Mare to wait for passersby, rare at that time of the morning, who could tell them where they could find via della Raganella (they meant della Reginella).

It was irresistible to some of the young soldiers finding themselves with a motor vehicle at their disposal, even if it was full of rounded-up Jews, to take a tour of the city. So that before reaching the detention center, the poor souls

standing inside the trucks had to suffer the most caprici-
ous peregrinations—always more uncertain of their des-
tination, and at every new turn, at every new street that
they traveled, assailed by various and always alarming conjectures. Naturally, the most popular goal of these tour-
ists was St. Peter's Square, where several trucks stopped
for long periods of time. While the Germans uttered the
Wunderbars with which they would sprinkle the tales they
intended to tell their Lili Marleens back home, from within
the truck came shouts and invocations to the pope, asking that he intercede, that he come to their aid. Then the
trucks were on their way again, and even that last hope
was gone.

The Jews were gathered at the Military College. The trucks
entered the grounds and drove to the furthest arcade. The
unloading operations were carried out as summarily and
roughly as the loading had been. The new arrivals were
made to line up in groups of three at some distance from
others like them, who were now under the surveillance
of numerous German guards, armed to the teeth. Several
Italian Fascist republicans were seen walking among the
groups with the arrogant scowls of inspectors and smug
festival-day airs.

Beginning at a certain time, the men and women were
separated and led into the halls of the college. It was dark
as the grave within because the blinds were hermetically
sealed. As far off as the courtyard, where the most dreadful confusion reigned all day long, one could hear anxious
screams mixed with mournful cries of suffering coming
from those halls. Every once in a while a threatening shout

in Italian reestablished a momentary and almost more anguished silence. It didn't take long, as in all places so jam-packed with people, for the place to become contaminated with stagnant air, like the miasma which affects all prisons and places of deportation. Guards and overseers almost always impeded the way to the latrines. The goal of humiliating, demoralizing, reducing these people to human rags, without will, almost without self-respect, was quickly evident.

Perhaps the Germans weren't expecting such utter success. The abundance of material rounded up exceeded their expectations, at least to judge by the site in which they had chosen to gather it, which, it soon became clear, was inadequate. And it was necessary to leave a large number of people, who couldn't be accommodated in the halls, under the arcade. The sturdiest-looking men, those who might threaten an "uprising" were placed with their faces toward the wall, which is by now the classic position for humiliation and intimidation, created by the Nazis from their first persecution of the Jews. If some child tried to play, the guards ordered the mother to make it stop, with the usual threat of shooting. Straw mattresses were set out and the order given to lie down on them.

During the night two women went into labor. The Italian doctors discerned that both would be difficult births requiring medical assistance. For these women the clinic would have been a road to freedom. But the Germans would not permit moving them, and the two newborns opened their eyes in the shadows of the ill-omened courtyard. What names were given to these two first-borns into a new Babylonian slavery? (Moses named the son born to him of Zipporah, while in servitude, Gershom, [wayfarer in a strange land], but the two born that night without a Moses were on their way to gas chambers.)

On the other hand, permission was obtained for a young boy who had a suppurating abscess to have it treated at the hospital. However, the Germans attended the surgical procedure, and as soon as it was over, took the boy back with them.

That's how Saturday night went by, then all day Sunday and Sunday night. The city and the Ghetto, in the meantime, had learned where the unfortunate souls had been taken. Relatives, passing themselves off as "Aryan" friends, came to the doors of the college, handed over food and notes for the prisoners, but never knew whether these comforts reached those for whom they were intended.

Toward dawn on Monday, the prisoners were boarded onto motor vans and taken to the Rome Tiburtino station, where they were loaded onto cattle cars, which remained on a dead-end siding the entire morning. Some twenty German armed guards prevented anyone from approaching the convoy.

At 1:30 P.M. the train was assigned to motorman Quirino Zazza. Almost immediately he realized that the cattle cars "contained"—so a relative of his put it—"many civilians mixed as to age and sex, who, he later realized, were of the Jewish race."

The train began moving at 2 P.M. A young woman, arriving from Milan to meet relatives in Rome, says that at Fara Sabina (but more likely at Orte) she passed the "sealed train" from which hellish cries were coming. There, through the grates of one of the cars, it seemed to her she recognized the face of a little girl related to her. She tried to call to the child, but another face came to the grating and signaled her to be quiet. This call to silence, to forgo any attempt to return them to human contact, is the last word, the last sign of life that we have from them.

Near Orte the train encountered a closed semaphore signal and had to stop for about ten minutes. "At the request of the confined passengers" (it is again the engineer who is speaking), several of the cars were opened, so "those who needed to take care of bodily functions could do so." There were several escape attempts, immediately terminated by ample gunfire.

At Chiusi, another short stop, to drop off the body of an old woman who had died during the trip. At Florence, Signor Zazzi left the train without having succeeded in speaking with anyone of those whom he had taken on the first step of the journey of deportation. With a change of service personnel, the train continued on to Bologna.

Neither the Vatican, nor the Red Cross, nor the Swiss, nor any other neutral state succeeded in obtaining information about the deportees. It is estimated that the number of those taken on October 16 alone was more than a thousand, but certainly the true figure must be higher, because many families were taken in their entirety, leaving no trace of themselves, nor any relatives or friends to report their disappearance.

Eight Jews

■ ■ ■ ■ ■ ■ ■ ■ ■ ■ ■

1. The Corvette Claymore

Rome, March 24, 1944. They are working on the so-called preliminary list for the Ardeatine Caves.[1] The Germans, on their own, had already taken ten hostages.

"I told Carretta to take ten names off. Eight Jewish names were at the very end of it. We figured they'd been added at the last minute in order to get the total to fifty. So Carretta took them off along with two others we chose at random."

These, according to newspaper accounts, were the words used by Raffaele Alianello, Commissioner for Public Security, expressly released from a concentration camp to testify as a witness before the High Court of Justice for the Punishment of Fascist Crimes in the Caruso trial. It is a well-known fact that policemen's

---

1. See Introduction, p. 10. (All notes are translator's.)

brains operate on a very simple level. Yet, in the perfor-
mance of his duties, especially in the eyes of his victims, a
policeman may appear to be diabolically clever, insightful,
a veritable psychologist! What wild flashes of imagination
and satanic inventions—the quickness and perspicacity of a
mind reader, of a radiographer of the soul. What bravura!
A consummate Thespian moving from pathos to cyni-
cism, from sympathetic, paternal kindliness to glacial fe-
rocity! But that kind of malignant intelligence is not in-
nate to a policeman. Quite the opposite, it is bestowed
upon him and comes from two sources: a bestowal, so to
speak, from beneath, in the sense that his victim, reduced
to a state of passivity, projects his own suppressed intelligence onto his tormentor and ascribes it to him; it is the
victim's panic which takes over the policeman's person and
endows it with the victim's own morbid fantasies, the pat-
terns of his obsessions, and the subtleties of his own fears.
And there's a bestowal from above, in the sense that the intelligence by which the police officer subjectively feels
himself spurred on is nothing but an investiture descend-
ing through the ranks from some inaccessible "Him."
One hardly dares allude to "Him" except by a sly upwards
thrust of the thumb over one's shoulder. And one hardly
dares whisper his name. Each police officer believes in and
relies on his own immediate superiors, who, in turn believe
in and rely on their superiors, and so on up the chain to the
Chief. And this Dark-Room King, this Doctor Mabuse,[2]

---

2. Dr. Mabuse, protagonist of a 1922 Fritz Lang silent film,
Dr. Mabuse, the Gambler, was a mad criminal and master of disguise
intent on taking over the world. In 1933 Lang directed a "talkie"
sequel, *The Testament of Dr. Mabuse.*

who makes sure that there is no clear return trail to mark his identity, gives the impression of being omnipotent—unpunishable since he goes unpunished—and capable of procuring immunity. "This is the art of not allowing one's self to be known," says the tyrant Holofernes in Hebbel's *Judith*,[3] "of always remaining a mystery." And it is the basic rule for the establishment of tyrannies and reigns of terror.

This was quite clearly seen in Germany when the Nazis took over the country. The minions mimicked the efforts and each and every expedient of their leaders, who in turn mimicked those of Hitler, who spoke of a mysterious drawer, in which he had locked away a socioeconomic plan for the regeneration of the Reich. Rauschning[4] showed us that the drawer was empty. At the base of every tyranny or reign of terror there's that empty drawer. The apparent intelligence and capacities of its agents—its policemen's shrewdness, its soldiers' daring—depend on a belief in that drawer.

Having opened the drawer and found it empty, even Alianello regressed into natural simplicity. Probably he thought it out like this. "It's not only the officers of the High Court and the few invited spectators who are following Caruso's—my ex-chief's—trial, but public opinion in all of Italy and, in a certain sense, the entire world. How

---

3. Christian Friedrich Hebbel (1813–1863), a German dramatist, wrote *Judith* in 1840.

4. Herman Rauschning, head of the Free State of Danzig, who joined the Nazi party in 1931, broke with it in 1934, and almost immediately began writing works exposing Hitler's true intentions.

many eyes are watching us! And the worst of it is that things are going badly these days. Today there's the concentration camp, tomorrow, who knows! Come on now! Let's find a way to make those eyes indulgent, impress them favorably. It's not likely we'll get another chance like this. But the first shot has to be right on target. And there's no time to lose. We have to provide instant, convincing, incontrovertible, palpable, yet indirect evidence that while evil people were collaborating with the "Nazi-Fascists," we, on the other hand, were among the good. But basically that's a simple problem. What was black yesterday has become white today, and vice versa. What was the most conspicuous feature of Fascism? Its calling card, so to speak? Its fingerprint? There you go! Persecution of Jews. Therefore, what is the most characteristic indication of anti-Fascism? Protection of Jews. When the Fascists were in charge of things, they condemned, worse, punished any benevolence toward Jews. Let's show ourselves as sympathetic, of having had such courage, and we'll immediately be admitted, officially admitted, without the slightest challenge, into the ranks of anti-Fascists. Let's go, fellow! Latch on to the Jews, everything goes into our soup, even forsworn meat. Make it look as if you threw a rope of kindness, as if acting out of kindness you gave preferential treatment to Jews."

Having concluded his silent thinking, the witness speaks. And sworn to tell the truth, the whole truth, nothing but the truth, he speaks the following words, which he believes, and correctly so, will be unforgettable. *"Immediately, the first thing I did with the preliminary list for the Ardeatine Caves was to cross off the names of eight Jews."*

Within himself, Alianello is rubbing his hands together. He's got them all—High Court, spectators, Italian public opinion, and world opinion—if not quite backed against the wall, certainly very close to it. The storm cloud of suspicion and prejudice that was surrounding him is now disappearing, becoming tinged with shades of soft pink; like one of those clouds that resemble swans or cherubs in flight.

The saving of human lives and the lives of innocents is the kind of deed which no subsequent error or frailty can diminish. Certainly the testimony of the witness Alianello during the trial on the 20th of September reflects on the act of Commissioner Alianello on March 24, but it is superimposed on it in a way that is, at the very least, ambiguous. Let's examine this superimposition from a Jewish perspective. The reactions it induces are mixed and complex. It gives Jews the feeling they are aboard the corvette *Claymore*, about which Victor Hugo writes in his novel *Ninety-Three*. Through the negligence of a sailor, the ship is in danger of being wrecked. But with superhuman courage and disdain for his own life, the sailor redeems his error and saves the ship. The Marchese of Lantenac decorates the man for valor and then immediately has him executed.

It's likely there were, it's likely there still are, plenty of Alianellos. It's likely they were even more numerous here in Rome, where one can say there isn't a Jewish family of which, on returning after all these months, one wouldn't be afraid to inquire about closest kin. Too many times already, we've come across closed, severe faces which forbid themselves any expression as superfluous and out of proportion to what they lived through. *Taken, deported, that morning of October 16. Never another word about them.* Still, that "never another word" is a benign euphemism, a disconsolate ray of hope striving to give the lie to the presages, the fears, perhaps to the certainty of the worst of all evils. It's likely there were Alianellos in Warsaw and in Lublin, on the railroad platforms from which the sealed cars and carriages left and still leave, their cargo no longer human beings, but tormented bodies, moans and cries: and in the cities, where in some elegant and out-of-the-way streets, deaf, dumb, and apparently functionless buildings, houses with closed shutters, hide torture chambers in their cellars. It's likely they were, likely they still are there, wherever Nazism is still committing carnage. Blessed are the Alianellos and cursed be anyone who would deduct even one iota from the gratitude that they deserve.

The mixed emotions of Jews in the face of Alianello's self-defense cannot even be discounted as the normal reaction of someone who, without knowing it, and without having permitted it, finds himself as reduced to being one of two cards (although the preferred one, the wild joker), in a duplicitous game; that is, to being and feeling oneself merely a playing card. This particular deceit, so highly acclaimed at first hearing, in the heat of the moment, as they say, is every day more and more appropriately discredited. Among other things, it has the defect of aspiring to surreptitiously reintegrate the ways of villainous ambiguity, double-faced cunning, and of the-end-justifies-the-means, with all honors, even decking them out in an aura of civic merit. And now, just when we've all had enough of Mussolini as Machiavelli! The world has finally earned the right to feel itself cleansed, and while it's in the very act of rebirth, along come the heroes of this game of playing both ends against the middle, doing their best to reset within its foundation the very kind of machination which could only have been devised on the whirlagig of the corrupted and corrupters, whose password, whose symbol were the words (forgive the expression) "take them all for suckers."

But all this still relates to morality in general and falls within the realm of public life. We've said that we want to take a specifically Jewish point of view. However, we also reject the alternative hypothesis: that the reluctance to owe something to an Alianello, and to being dragged into court with him, to testify as a witness in his defense, can only be ascribed in a thousand-year-leap to arrogant and stiff-necked Semitic pride.

For several centuries Jews have been plagued by a dreadful prototype, all the more treacherous because created by a superb poet, who bestowed upon it his own gift of immortality. And in it, he has compressed old and new anti-Semitic accusations and suspicions from ritual homicides, if one may employ such an expression, to that of exorbitant and inexorable usury. This is the personage of Shylock. (*The Merchant of Venice* was revived during the last years of Fascism by an astute theater manager, who today is a collaborationist, to pay homage to the racial campaign with glorious flattery.) One easily fails to see that Shylock is responding to the torments of paternal love betrayed, of honor and family feelings trampled. On the contrary, Shylock is seen as nothing more than "the Jew," the Jewish merchant, who doesn't listen to reason, who claims, demands, insists on being paid a pound of living flesh from his insolvent debtor's body.

Hurt by this ancient denunciation, which every pro-
scenium in the world has tirelessly revived to the proper
scorn of audiences, and which the shelves of every library in the world disseminate every day, what emotions
can Jews feel when they are forced to accept the fact that
Shylock is not only an insult but an outrageous injury—
that too often it is precisely they who fall victim to ever new
incarnations and unforseeable variations of Shylock? And
now when within the free countries the light begins to
shine for them again, and every morning on waking, they
ask themselves whether the air they are breathing is truly
the air of this world, here comes a new Shylock, firm in
his own claim, to ask not for a piece of living flesh, but
for passive complicity in demonstrating his purity, and his
faultless anti-Fascist faith. If they had the mind to make
jokes about it, Jews might very well ask, "Who in the offensive meaning of the word, in its rapacious connotation,
is the real Jew?"

It is likely that the Alianello case has no bearing on anything else. Still, it is a symptom. And to the not-yet-healed
sensibilities of Jews, it says that the racial campaign is not
over. *Persecution continues.* We know the response—that
this is a morbid hypersensitivity which we need to get over;
that it's talmudic pedantry, and a corrosive taste for paradox, ancient Jewish diseases. If it were a morbid sensibility,
that is, an indication of a rather unsociable state of mind,
we would apologize for it. If it should seem to be talmudic pedantry, we say that Alianello's ostensible excuse
was neither solicited, nor enlarged upon, because of a fool-
ish passion for casuistry. It may indeed be an excuse, but
one that allows us to speak our minds to both sides, to

those whom the Fascists call Aryans, and to ourselves as well. As for its being a paradox, we deny it, and will try to demonstrate the point.

2. The Ghetto and Noah's Ark

This is the situation that Commissioner Alianello and his colleague were facing: a list of sixty names, of which ten were superfluous. Therefore, ten people to be saved. Saved, if one can so describe it, legally, within the limits of the *Diktat,* without earning merit, but also without risk. All sixty were equally innocent. In similar situations one chooses lots. It's the customary rule that follows right after "women and children first" in fires, shipwrecks, floods, and other such catastrophes. Even Alianello was a child at one time. It seems impossible to us now, but even he must have frolicked and played in the fields of infancy. And even he must have sung, as we all do, the old nursery rhyme about the little boat that can no longer stay afloat—and how they choose straws on the little boat to see who will survive. Didn't he think of it on the afternoon of March 24? Certainly he must have. The proof is that he and his colleague, after having already removed the eight Jews, chose the other two names "at random" (words from his own testimony).

Why did the Jews merit privilege, take precedence? Why of ten exemptions did they get eight? The injustice was equal for all. It doesn't matter that the other prisoners were being held for specific charges and that their sentences, even without that act of reprisal, had already been decided and meted out. First of all, if two names were chosen at random, then the other eight could have been chosen at random. Second, the Jews were subject to the racial accusations, which under the Nazis were nothing to be taken lightly.

But to Alianello the Jews must have seemed the most innocent of the innocent, the most unjust victims of unjust victims. Not for nothing had Fascist propaganda exposed them to years of execration and extermination. Not for nothing had, all the years of the racial campaign, the characteristic iniquity of reactionary dictatorships, been its supreme infamy, so that the oppression of the Jews was the first wrong that had to be righted; so that reparations for Jews would have to be almost the first symbol of a resurgence, of freedoms restored to all. People like Alianello, petty bourgeois, susceptible, credulous, arrogant, impressionable, excitable, with law degrees, well enough advanced to believe in ideas but not enough to have any of their own—such people are the most pliable material for propaganda. They are ardent converts to every publicity campaign, proselytes of slogans. In preferentially saving Jews with an eye to possible future credit to himself, Alianello was following an advertising campaign, like someone who buys the most publicized toothpaste, expecting that his teeth will be whiter the next morning. He was obeying a slogan.

Had he at least said "we cast lots and came up with eight Jews." But no, he emphasized his deliberate choice. Another deliberate choice. A reparative "campaign" to reverse a destructive "campaign." Nevertheless, a campaign. Under the Nazis, Jews felt, and still feel themselves, either the subject, predicate, nominative, accusative, or dative of murderous slogans: "Let's get rid of the Jews. Let's exterminate the Jews." Among people who are on the way to regaining freedom, they find themselves once again, and with a striking parallelism, the accusative or the dative of a benevolent slogan. "Let's save the Jews. Let's compensate the Jews." Dative or accusative, grammatical analysis tells us these are merely "cases." What troubles Jews and makes them uncomfortable is precisely their remaining "a case"—eternally, irremediably the Jewish case. A slogan encloses them as does a Ghetto, even if, by chance, it looks like Noah's Ark. They are thrown into it, jammed in indiscriminately without regard to their faults or merits, their vices or virtues, without any notion of them as— we won't even say the word individuals—merely human beings.

Persecuted, proscribed, murdered, not for their ideas or their behavior, but because they have a collective identity as a "race," even their benefactors, when the time comes to save them, do not range them with other human beings of equal risk and fortune. No, they save them en masse, as the almost anonymous representatives, no better defined, than as members of a "race." Grammatical particles. Hitler, Mussolini, and Alianello.

The heart, as we know, has its reasons, which take precedence over reason, and even over the pleasure of being right. Rejected lovers ask for, if not love, at least hate. The heart feels itself alive only when it is the object of specific and animated emotions. This gives it, so to speak, its self-respect. Did Mussolini hate Jews? All we know is that in 1938 he traded them for a closer alliance with

Hitler. He traded in Jews as though they were cash. He pronounced their fate with his jaw stuck out as he was wont to do with the important topic in his tirades. He was acting out a moment of international demagoguery. Does Alianello love Jews? We know that at the Caruso trial he traded them to cleanse and purify his own political record—a matter of anti-Fascist demagoguery. Just as with Mussolini, Jews didn't feel themselves the objects of a sincere, passionate, physical hatred, so with the commissioner-rescuer, they didn't feel themselves the beneficiaries of a true, committed, charitable, or, to put it plainly, Christian love.

Well, so what do these Jews want? Hatred? Are they dying for persecution based on genuine detestation? Are they permitting themselves the luxury of such masochism in these times? All they have to do is apply to the Germans. But even in that case, apart from Hitler's hysteria, apart from the old and new cavils of traditional German anti-Semitism, it was immediately evident—and Trotsky explained it back in 1933[5]—that Hitler, having to cheat the German proletariat of class warfare, in exchange presented them with the racial campaign. Jews were the first "surrogates" in a Reich of surrogates. They were an instrument of social demagoguery.

It seems to me that of all the humiliating jobs, being a sandwich man must be one of the most demeaning. Those

---

5. Leon Trotsky, an early associate of Lenin, broke with Russian revolutionists and was assassinated in Mexico in 1940. In the spring of 1933 while in exile in Turkey, he wrote a series of essays on the state of German National Socialism.

wretched souls go about parading placards bearing garish, cartoonish, and often stupid ads for products that have nothing to do with them and which, most likely, they know nothing about. Perhaps Jews, forced to go around marked with armbands or yellow stars, and other contrivances for identification in countries where persecution was most severe, felt a little like sandwich men. And in fact they too were serving as publicists in a demagogic campaign totally alien to them. With the difference that sandwich men earn a living thereby, and Jews earn death.

We all know about people who carry diseases. One day the pediatrician turns up at your house, swabs your children's throats, and after 24 to 48 hours telephones you to say that upon examination the presence of diphtheria bacilli has been established. Thank heaven the children are well. In their exuberant good health, they mock the idea of spots in their throats, of high fever, and injections of antitoxins. But the invisible diphtheria bacilli are playing hide and seek in the game room. So in the meanwhile, the children are declared to be "carriers" and are quarantined. And they besiege you with questions. They don't understand how you can be sick when you are well. So too, Jews, more or less unexpectedly, had been declared carriers. In vain they sought the germ they were accused of harboring, and in vain looked about for anyone they might have infected. The "others" around them were glowing with good health. The "others" were feeling so powerful that they even wanted to pick fights, exhaust themselves in the most violent sports. And in fact, shortly thereafter, they started the war. From the moment when there was no way to escape their persecution, Jews tried to find its causes, to at least understand their persecutors' reasons. Identifying the logic of it, even in part, would have been a way of alleviating their suffering. For all their good intentions, they never succeeded.

What was their vice, what the sin, that so inexorably turned them into a public peril? Persecutions of the past can still be viewed almost as if they were local wars. In those days Jews, willingly or not, comprised a single cell, an enclosed nucleus, a specific social group, which easily antagonized the others—resembling a gypsy clan camped at the edge of a city, provocative because of the strangeness and difference of its customs, offensive because of that very insularity and isolation to which it's been constrained—who then declare war on it with edicts and sticks. But in this era? It was necessary to reconstruct an abstract of the group known as "Jews" through the use of scientific methodology; then to merge them all into that group, stripping them of their individuality, of the world in which they lived, of their habits, work, businesses, their practical and spiritual interchanges, tearing them out by their roots, no matter the damage of that extirpation, not only for the uprooted, but for the soil in which they had been flourishing. The abstraction such an operation involves is also evident in the work required to accomplish it, dull work with statistics, registries, censuses, forms, declarations, records and documents, boxes, long and short columns of numbers. We repeat, it wasn't a group of human beings they separated out. They created a group out of grammatical terms to make a powerful propaganda statement.

Digression: How Jews feel about their Judaism is a question not easily answered. At all events it is an extremely personal matter. There is no denying that there are deep internal and individual ways of feeling oneself Jewish. But these are private feelings, bounded by a sense of modesty, and never publicly demonstrated by deed. Therefore they do not affect the social behavior of a person, nor distinguish him from others, far less set him in opposition to others. (If you want to split hairs, you might say that, if there is a difference, it is only in the effort not to differentiate oneself, which can often become unpleasant. However, it is more disturbing to the person constrained to behave in that way, than to the person who had in some way provoked that behavior. And in no case is it anything that can upset world order or threaten the foundations of society.) To feel oneself Jewish means to hear again deeply within oneself—during hours of the most intimate reflection, hours so intimate that they are almost inexpressible— the old synagogue melodies heard in one's childhood during the endless monotony of oppressive twilights, while faint reflections of candlelight flicker on the cantor's biretta as he stands alone on the empty tabernacle. And upon hearing that chanting, one's soul turns to a wandering search of lost time,[6] the desolation upon facing miseries without end, the burning of poorly dried tears, the trembling of hopeless smiles, an embrace of shades from nether lands, the poignant recognition of ancestors one has never known, a secret inexpressible melancholy, and tireless prostrations before invisible wailing walls. Ah,

---

6. *A la recherche de le temps perdu* (In search of lost time) is the title of Marcel Proust's great novel. Debenedetti was one of Italy's and Europe's earliest champions of Proust.

thought no longer flies on golden wings, no longer alights on rises and hills.[7] By the river Babylon, on the path of willows, the eternal wanderer will perhaps find his way; and come to an ancient passage, an ancestral sign to lead him down to the region of the Mothers,[8] so that he can proceed on to question the "mouth of shadow." And in this too we clearly see a personal equation between man and Nature, between man and God; never a personal equation between man and society, between man and modern history. And moreover none of these were things which in any way could be blamed on the Jews. So Jews went on wondering in what and where their guilt lay.

An open-minded and very humane writer has aptly described the monstrosity of the racial laws, observing that they punished "not the accountable behavior of a human being, but the crime of being born." And who, of those who truly atoned for that crime with death, has yet returned to tell us whether in their time of torment, they finally understood their guilt? Certainly the persecutors had been able to create gas chambers and every other of the most brutal techniques for murder; the kinds that cause one to die with a contorted face, with lips set in a scream and a curse, that deprive dying of its supernatural com-

---

7. "Va, pensiero": "Fly thought on golden wings/fly, alight on rises and hills," is sung by a chorus of Israelites recalling their lost homeland in Giuseppe Verdi's opera *Nabucco* (*Nebuchadnezzar*). One of opera's most famous choruses, it became a kind of national anthem during Italy's struggle for unification, and again when the country was under German occupation.

*8. In Part II of Goethe's *Faust*, Mephistopheles gives Faust a key which will lead him "to the deepest of all realms: to see the Mothers."

pensations and promises, of at least peace and silence, of comforting visions of Limbo or Elysium, with grass beneath one's feet and blue skies above. In the ghastly sweats and chills of death throes, writhing more horribly than from asphyxia itself, those poor unfortunates might well have cursed the long-ago nuptials in which their parents' love had been joined: ill-omened marriages, which filled their mothers' wombs with the seeds of those accursed monsters now writhing in one of those suffocating death chambers. And the stench of gas will have putrefied the spring nuptials in which fathers and mothers had exchanged their first loving glances. Perhaps just then, in these deliriums, the crime of having been born resulted in an accusation against those who had brought them into the world, as is said to happen during outbursts by children of syphilitics and tabetics, conceived in a moment of sordid and infected lust. For a second, the buried feeling of sin might rise again through generations. But it was a curse torn from them by torture and to have torn out that curse is, for Nazis, a true masterwork.

Peace to our dead. But for the living, who never understood and still do not understand the reason for their persecution, alarm is the appropriate reaction today to the gift of this unearned indulgence. This shutting of the eyes and creating exceptions and advantages for Jews is not a way of redressing wrongs. Proper redress would be to set Jews once again amid other people's lives, in the circle of all human fate, and not to segregate them, even for benevolent reasons. This is anti-persecution, and therefore created of the same psychological and moral substance as persecution. If, formerly, Jews were punished for their Jewishness, on viewing the current situation, not at all corrected, but simply stood on its head, with perfect antithetical symmetry, it gives rise to the suspicion that Jews are being forgiven for their Jewishness. Forgiveness recalls the concept of guilt, of transgression. Here they are again, these Jews, once again at risk of having to set off on a torturous, insoluble, offensive search for a reason. And then, faced with historical recurrences, which unfortunately, are in their memory, it is legitimate to ask, "Pardon or amnesty? And how long will it last?" We will explain this with an example!

3. Farmers of the Volcano

We were returning from Naples in pouring rain, sitting atop a truckload of walnuts. A strange-looking fellow had come on board with us; three days worth of beard, with evasive ways as though he were a fugitive, yet his ragged clothes still revealed their middle-class quality, and everything else about him, his face, his expression, and mien were middle-class as well. Until a few years ago, everyone in his household must have called him "the young master." The ex-young master threw a briefcase, from which a long roll protruded, on top of all the suitcases. "Tuna roe," he told us, and never stopped repeating, "I mustn't lose it or I'll be ruined." A fledgling black marketeer, we thought, maybe a middle-class professional, whom the stringency of the times has forced into this new profession so incongruous to the Trivium and Quadrivium.[9] With

---

9. The Liberal Arts: The Trivium consisted of grammar, rhetoric and logic. The Quadrivium consisted of arithmetic, geometry, music and astronomy.

utmost kindness, he enquired the name of each of his companions, their family situation, address, and whether their children were boys or girls; almost as if trying with this sketchy kind of friendship, to ingratiate himself with them, to seek their protection for himself, who was so out of his element, so inexpert. Naive, almost pathetic. Later, at a barricade we learned that this naïf is a young police official, returning from a short leave in his home town of Palermo. The fellow is suddenly completely metamorphosed. It's superfluous; "Right you are, if you think you are," is still a great psychological insight, and Sicily keeps proving her Pirandello correct. Therefore all the specious game of inquiries, questions, investigations on the part of that character so in search of an author, was nothing but a training session for future interrogations, voluntary propaedeutica in the art of worming information out of other people, exercises done on the five black keys so that when he is seated behind the large harpsichord of his police desk, he will be able to perform the most virtuosic preludes, the most Lisztian accompaniments, to get his chickens to squeal. In particular then, almost as if our faces were so many mirrors, the man studied the effects in them of certain facial expressions; a kind of sideways glance as if through the lenses of nonexistent eyeglasses, a sly, furtive look, gentle yet accusatory at the same time, a glance that seemed to say, "Talk to me! What's the use of hiding our cards from each other?"

When our turn came, and without a moment's hesitation we stated our name, that young and passionate Dominican of police inquisitions, that future repopulator of Italian prisons, started with triumph, as when in the glory days of his future career, the thoughtless response of some poor wretch would allow him to link together at lightning speed a complicated chain of inductions, to suddenly seize upon an inert mass of evidence and produce a clear indictment, and in an instantaneous dramatic stroke, to conclude a series of inquiries which had promised to be long and difficult. "Debenedetti? A Jew?" he burst out. And immediately there was that professional glance from behind nonexistent eyeglasses sweeping up at us, flashing obliquely, resolving into a turbulent look of overlapping implications, inferences, of involuntary and almost repugnant complicity, of sullen tolerance. "Well, this time you've gotten away with it," is what the look said, "thanks only to the amnesty. Get going now, old fox, but watch out that we don't get our hands on you again. That 'wanted' look on your face is something not even God in Heaven can wipe off." It might make us seem nasty if we added that his look also contained a shade, a trace, the barest hint of regret. "If only we had caught you out like this a few months ago."

It is not morally true, nor is it plausible, that the revocation of an order, ipso facto, results in the revocation of the habit of following it. The new order has to mature in order to actually become the new order. And there isn't anyone who expects that the world, this world which was created in seven days, can be changed in one hour. Otherwise, how can we trust that one additional hour—whenever it might come—wouldn't be enough for it to relapse into its worst form and return to its own vomit? The exclamation, the look in our little policeman's eyes exposed the effort of adapting to a different way of looking at things, the necessary though rapid maneuver required to reverse a current. We suspect that the new way of looking at things is likely to be adopted as if it were an order from above; a kind of decree promulgated by the Official Gazette, and therefore by its very nature subject, as well, to revocation dictated by the necessity of the moment . . . seeing that . . . in consideration of. . . . The suspicion here is that our little police officer was conforming to today's principles with yesterday's mentality, keeping an eye on that omnipotent, inexorable, and obscure Divinity, known as "political sensitivity" in whose name yesterday's functionaries, journalists, high- and low-ranking officials are elevated or ousted. Order of the day, "Show sympathy to Jews."

But anyone, who, like Jews, thirsts for liberty—one of those thirsts that cling to the palate—anyone who has understood that Liberty is literally a question of life or death, is ready to recognize that included within all the liberties that constitute Liberty, is *the liberty to be anti-Semitic.* An anti-Semitism of free men, a liberal anti-Semitism (if that isn't a contradiction), against which one could pose valid arguments and pertinent refutations, would seem almost stimulating, revitalizing, regenerating to the Jewish people, who are just now emerging from the restrictions of immobility and silence. To finally speak out in the open, measure oneself, think things through for themselves as men among men, men confronting other men, would seem too good to be true to them, who until yesterday had been forced to hide themselves, suppress their reactions and responses, change their identities, fearing even to speak their own names, or, to put it simply, to call themselves their fathers' sons.

In his review of Wendell L. Wilke's *One World,* Benedetto Croce took the occasion to reassert the "fundamental need of mankind to suffer and work."[10] Now, at this time in the war, and after many years, Jews are again finding public acceptance of their need to work. And the need to suffer is wholly reborn in them. Haven't they suffered enough? Of course they've suffered—the world knows how much—and there beyond the front lines of Liberty, they are still suffering, and to such an extent that this claim of ours to suffering might seem like sacrilege, ugly defiance, provocation of fate. But on closer study the claim's sole purpose is not to assert title to, nor to see ourselves accorded, any special rights. The right to not have special rights. Special, meaning racial.

What Jews would prefer is that the sufferings of those of them presently liberated and of those still being persecuted, be poured into, mixed, mingled with the long collective, the common levy of tears and pleas that all humans worthy of the name have sacrificed, and are still sacrificing, to assure the world its longest period of civilized centuries. If there is a right that Jews claim, it is only this: that those of their dead who died of violence and hunger, their infants who, after months of starvation in their places of hiding, didn't survive the first sip of milk finally offered to them, their women kicked and machine-gunned to death, their newborns tossed in the air and gunned down as though they were birds, should be ranked with all the other dead—all the other victims of this war. They too were soldiers, alongside every other soldier.

---

10. Wendell Wilke ran against Franklin D. Roosevelt for president of the United States in 1940. Croce (1866–1952) was internationally known as a literary critic and philosopher.

Their uniforms were their everyday clothes, stripped away by sufferings, useless on their skeletal bodies. Some of them were even armed—the children, who were clutching rag dolls and tin guns, considered unworthy playthings for German children. Thus, they marched toward their front lines, which were places of affliction and torture. They too disembarked, but on the shores of the beyond. Fallen forward, their faces—those features that editors of many "defenders of the race" publications had photographed to slap on the covers of their filthy publications—with eyes that no one closed—did not look toward the high and distant sky. These soldiers ask only that the places of their slaughter be recorded among the battlefields of this war. They ask that at a roll call of the dead their names be included among those of other soldiers who have fallen in the war—without any added glory, which, by wronging their comrades in arms, would offend the cause of justice for which they died, the fraternity of the dead, and would seem a wrong done to them. Without the addition of pity—pity for the poor Jews, which would debase their sacrifice.

And if, some day, there is a desire to reward the valor of these dead, we Jewish survivors will certainly not refuse it. But don't strike a special medal for them, don't print special awards. Let them be the medals and awards of all the other soldiers. *Soldier Coen, Soldier Levi, Soldier Abramovic, Soldier Chaim Blumenthal, age five, fell at Leopoli amid his family with his hands tied behind his back, while still defending and bearing witness to the cause of liberty.* We, the unworthy survivors, will listen to these calls, standing at attention, trying not to tremble as we clasp the hand extended toward us. Our voices will strain to be steady when we reply, "Thank you, General." Then we will return to the silent, interminable lines in which the families of all the other fallen, the whole world's mourners, are ranged in that solemn religious parade of humanity.

The need to suffer of which Croce speaks is nothing if not the need to feel oneself alive and among the living, to be a participant in the inevitable struggle and conflict that daily work and duties require in this world. If the world were to become an idyllic place, it would at that very moment become a world of the walking dead, no matter how deceptively glazed over and embellished it might be with the colors of life. That is why Jews request this honor of suffering—meaning they are asking not to be cheated, not even by way of indemnities or reparations—of their part in the heritage of all humanity. For centuries upon centuries they have preserved and repeated the message of the Old Testament, chanting it in their shadowy synagogues, during vigils and fasts, on Sabbaths and Days of Repentance, in the Ghetto and in the streets of the Diaspora. How would they have forgotten that the concept of bread, that is, of the very source and sustenance of life, is indissolubly tied to the concept of suffering, of the sweat of one's brow? They do not want an earthly paradise at the cost of breaking the rules.

It goes without saying that it is too easy to adapt oneself to privilege and advantage. A life of comfort affects memory, rendering it superficial, and confirming it in its already too spontaneous lability. We forget yesterday's suffering, including, and particularly, the most painful and bitter, and we forget the price we paid in grief and anguish for the comforts, which seem to have been bestowed on us precisely to help us forget. One becomes accustomed to being loved, to living with ease; the habit quickly risks becoming a need; and the acquired need risks creating the presumption of a right. This pattern of ours may seem a quarrelsome, peevish, self-pitying, implacable fear of being loved. But it is only the fear of being gratuitously loved, undeservedly loved; that is, wrongly loved; no longer obligated to do anything to merit that love. But tomorrow, inevitably, we will have to begin to earn it. And then? Won't we have become too spoiled?

It is not that Jews in these recent days have felt themselves the subjects of a too fulsome largesse of advantages, mere targets in a shooting gallery of benevolence. What we're talking about is a symptom, a possibility, about which we've garnered or sensed some indication. And it is this, as well, which acquits these remarks of any imputation of ingratitude. As we have stated, these observations are meant to be heard by all sides. What discomfort we felt, for example, when someone, laughing, though without malice, merely in appreciation of a psychological phenomenon, told the story of those Jews, who, on emerging from their hiding places at the arrival of the liberating armies, immediately, after the first words of greeting, declared themselves to be Jewish, as though it entitled them to special recognition, concessions, and compensation. It could even have been these very same people, who, during the Deluge, put together the most unseemly umbrellas for themselves, and did their utmost to eliminate any suspicion of "belonging to the race."

One evening, during the darkest time of the Deluge, Bernard Berenson[11] posed the eternal question. "Why do Jews remain Jews in the face of the cyclical return of persecutions?" And he answered himself with a Sicilian reminiscence. Once, long before, while touring the slopes below Mount Etna, he admired their Promised Land fecundity. One of the farmers, however, told him that the lava periodically descended and burned out those fields. "So why do you go on cultivating them?" he asked. "Because when good times return, your excellency, they are so good that they repay us for every misfortune." This, said the eminent writer, was an analogy that explained the tenacity and survival of the Jews.

On that bitter evening, the anecdote accomplished the desired goal, which was to comfort us and help us believe in the return of better times, to reconnect us to life by at least linking us to those farming the volcano. But Berenson will not mind if, now that the lava flow has retreated, his story pleases us a little less. What we would like to explain is that it's not as if Jews submit to the affliction of seven lean years just because they are expecting the recurrence of seven rich years. They are human beings certainly, and they too cherish security, comfort, even happiness. Lean years don't appeal even to them. But it doesn't follow, nor must it follow, that afterwards, in compensation, they expect extra-rich years. If for nothing else,

---

11. Berenson (1865–1959), a Lithuanian-born Jew who was educated in America and spent most of his adult life in Italy, became an international authority on Renaissance art.

for dignity, for a sense of fairness in life, for their human *amor fati*, love of chance and fate. Neither too lean, nor too rich. Something just right.

September 1944

The Fate of the Roman Jewish Libraries

■ ■ ■ ■ ■ ■ ■ ■ ■ ■ ■

Estelle Gilson

Among the outrages perpetrated against the Roman Jewish community immediately before the roundup was the seizure of its rabbinical and community libraries. The community library, though the smaller of the two, was by far the more valuable. Established in the first years of the twentieth century with materials collected from the Ghetto's oldest congregations of different rites—two Italian, two Spanish, and one Sicilian—from religious and educational societies dating back to the fifteenth and sixteenth centuries, and subsequently augmented by important collections, it was Italy's richest Jewish library in terms of rare and unique items. Debenedetti's ironic description early in *October 16, 1943*, of a crisply uniformed SS officer lavishing his attention upon this precious Jewish material, calls our notice to the devastating loss.

But this kind of outrage was not perpetrated only against Roman Jews. Jewish communities throughout Europe were looted not only of the splendid material objects which tempt untrained eyes, but of the less conspicuous yet more valuable objects of spiritual wealth: their books and archives—their very history.

What proved to be unique about the pillage of the Roman Jewish community library was that while most Jewish libraries were eventually located and recovered, at least in part, after the war—and though the core of the rabbinical library was returned to Rome—the fate of the community library has never been clearly established. To this day the library is still being sought.

The libraries were housed on the second and third floors of the community's building in locked bookcases with solid wooden doors. Two uniformed German officers, who declared themselves Orientalists—one, a captain, said he was a professor of Hebrew in Berlin—visited them for the first time on September 30, 1943. The men returned to the library the following day and on the day after that, October 2, went to the Chief Rabbi's home. Not finding him in, they forced his door and took away books and papers. On October 11 an SS officer attached to the German ambassadorial staff, accompanied by a civilian, returned to the community's offices, inspected the libraries once again, and telephoned Otto & Rosoni, a firm of carriers, to arrange transportation of the books. On learning that it would take several days to obtain the necessary freight cars, the Germans threatened the community secretary with death if any of the books were removed. On the 14th in the presence of a Captain Mayer, and of Ugo Foa,

president of the Jewish community, Rosina Sorani, its secretary, and Giorgio Sierra, its "shamash," (sexton) the community library located on the second floor of the building
and part of the rabbinical library on the third floor were
loaded into two waiting freight cars marked "DRPI
Munchen 97970 C" and "DRPI Munchen 97970 G."
Though the books, like all Holocaust victims, traveled
in sealed cars bound for Germany, they were carefully
treated—stacked in layers with corrugated sheets between
and packed in wicker cases. The loading operation took the
entire day. The German officer announced that he would
return the following week for the remainder of the books.
Perhaps he didn't know of the roundup scheduled for
just a few days later. Perhaps he intended to allay suspicion should any word of the roundup have leaked out. The
Germans did not turn up until two months later, on December 14, when finding the community offices closed,
they forced their way in and broke into the bookcases. On
December 21 they returned with a waiting railway car but
could not locate fuel for transportation. However, by December 23 the pillage of the libraries was complete.

The looting of cultural material was a specialty of
the Einsatzstab Reichsleiter Rosenberg (ERR) a "cultural
commando" unit established by Alfred Rosenberg, theo-
retician of Nazi Socialism. While most Nazis would have
assigned Jewish cultural material the same fate as they did
its people, history has made it poignantly clear that Jewish books had a far better survival rate than did Jewish
human beings. The collection and preservation of libraries
was Rosenberg's "pet project." He had earlier established
specialized centers throughout Germany where materials

were amassed for the study of various issues. The center for the "Jewish Question" was housed in Frankfort, in what was originally the Rothschild Library. With the Allied bombing of Frankfort, material housed there was moved to the village of Hungen. Here alone, by 1945, there were six different repositories housing 1,200,000 items. After the war a huge American effort was undertaken to locate the libraries, books, and archives that the ERR had scattered in hiding places throughout Germany and to return them to their original owners.

As an endless stream of material began pouring in, the restitution process, which was begun in the Rothschild Library, was moved to a factory in Offenbach that had housed the I. G. Farben works. The determination of most books' provenance could be made by their book plates or library stamps. But not all books were marked and there were untold thousands of unidentifiable manuscripts, loose documents, and papers. And even identifiable books and libraries could not be returned to now-dead owners and to Jewish communities that no longer existed. Book plates and stamps that passed through the Offenbach depot, however, were all photographed and are today part of the National Archives, making it possible to review these records.

The records indicate that the library of the Roman Jewish community did not pass through Offenbach. The widely circulated explanation in Rome for the library's disappearance was that the railroad car carrying it had been almost immediately struck by a bomb during an Allied air attack on Civitavecchia, just outside Rome.

The 7000-volume library had never been catalogued. Fabian Herskovits, a Hungarian Jew who was to undertake

Book Stamps of the Missing Roman Jewish Community Library.

the task in 1938, was forced to leave Italy when the racial laws were passed. The only listing of any of its holdings was prepared in 1934 by a Polish-born scholar and bibliographer, who took the name Isaia Sonne when he became an Italian citizen. Sonne's typewritten catalogue describes approximately 250 antiquarian works of special interest in five categories: *Manuscripts, Incunables* (works printed before 1501), *Soncinos* (works from the press founded in the fifteenth century by a Jewish family that took its name from the Italian town in which the press was founded), *Orientalia* (works from Eastern Europe and the Mediterranean basin), and *Miscellany.*

The Sonne catalogue is the backbone of a report on the library which the Roman Jewish community prepared in 1961 when it applied for reparations which it eventually received from the West German government for all its losses, including items from both libraries.

Some books escaped the pillage. A 1485 commentary on the Bible by David Kimchi survived by being hidden in a garden. A few early printed books escaped Nazi eyes in a synagogue safe. Some incunables turned up miraculously, in apparently unexamined cupboards in the rabbi's office. Ariel Toaff, writing in *La Bibliofilia* in 1978 about the library, noted that in 1963, during the course of preparations for an exhibition entitled *The Two Thousand Year History of the Jewish Community in Rome,* three other incunables came to light. Four more reappeared during subsequent reorganizations of the community's archives and library in the late 1970s. Of the fifteen surviving rare books cited by Professor Toaff, eight were among those listed in Sonne's catalogue.

Then, suddenly, there was renewed hope that the library might indeed still exist. In a 1998 interview in the Rome Jewish community's publication *Shalom,* Dr. Sandro Di Castro, president of the community, announced that two books bearing the library's stamp had been offered at auction in New York three years earlier, and that "authorities" had been called in to investigate the matter. Representatives of the German and Italian governments were asked to aid in a renewed search, and Di Castro pleaded for all the world, Jews in particular, to help locate the missing library. In November 1999, Fritjof von Nordenskjold, the German ambassador to Italy, informed Dr. Di Castro that, despite an intense search, the Jewish Museum in Frankfort could find no trace of the library's books. The ambassador suggested that the books might have passed through Offenbach and promised a search of the records of the German Office for Cultural Affairs.

In response to my own inquiry about the renewed search for the library in December 1999, Luciano Violante, president of the Italian Chamber of Deputies, cited past and present efforts of the Italian government in regard to the restoration of Jewish property and art stolen by the Nazis but offered no new information in regard to the library.

As of this writing, in September 2000, nothing has been learned about the books offered at auction; no one even seems to know their names. According to the community librarian, the report that the books had been offered at auction had come from an Italian scholar who had merely seen the books in passing. In a written message to me, the scholar denies making such a report.

At least two rare books that once belonged to the Jewish community library of Rome are in New York. Numbers 12 and 17 of the manuscripts described in Isaia Sonne's catalogue are at the Jewish Theological Seminary in New York. Both bear the Roman library's stamp on the outside of their vellum covers and the presentation plate of their American donor, Harry G. Friedman, inside their covers. Friedman was a major patron of the seminary, as well as of the Jewish Museum and the Metropolitan Museum of Art. According to present JTS librarian, Meyer G. Rabinowitz, the seminary acquired the book "in the 1960s." Although there was no specific reference to this acquisition in the correspondence between Friedman and the seminary's librarians of that era, the files give one an insight into how European Jewish cultural artifacts were bought and sold, and by whom, in the decades following the war.

Two other volumes bearing the Rome community library stamp, one a manuscript, the other an early printed book, *Yad Shearim,* issued in Rome in 1547, are reportedly in the library of Hebrew Union College in Cincinnati. Information about the manuscript was not specific enough to confirm this holding. However, the library does own a copy of *Yad Shearim* published in Rome in 1547, said to have been acquired in 1930, long before the Nazi looting took place. It is of interest, however, that Isaia Sonne left Italy in 1938 to join the faculty of the Hebrew Union College and eventually became its librarian. While in Italy he had dealt in antiquarian books (having learned the trade from Cecil Roth) and acquired his own collection of Hebraica and Judaica. Sonne died in 1960 and left his personal library to the Ben Zvi Institute in Israel.

What was the fate of the Roman Jewish community library? It might have been bombed, in which case any of its works existing elsewhere in the world would likely have been taken from it before 1943. Or it might, as some evidence suggests, have reached Munich's Institute for the History of New Germany. If, however, it arrived there in October 1943, it would have been the very moment that the institute's own collections were being moved for reasons of safety. The Roman library, therefore, may reside in an obscure corner of some German university or institute. Or it might, in the course of its travels, have fallen into the hands of a private collector, who, from time to time, tests the safety of the market.

A library stamp in or on a volume does not, nor should it, deter libraries from acquiring a rare and desired item. Rare book and manuscript libraries may receive items from private donors, but most acquisitions result from purchases from dealers or at auction. "The primary suppliers" for the library of the Jewish Theological Seminary, according to Dr. Rabinowitz, "are public auctions both here and in Israel." Auctioneers and librarians uniformly affirm that the provenance of an item must be clearly and satisfactorily established, before a purchase can be consummated.

It is not easy, however, to establish provenance in this unique market. One reason, according to Benjamin Richler, director of the Jerusalem-based Institute of Microfilmed Hebrew Manuscripts, is that the past 150 years have witnessed the dispersal of important collections of Hebrew manuscripts. In his 1994 *Guide to Hebrew Manuscript Collections,* Richler cites some of the problems that have made the institute's task of locating, collecting, and microfilming this material so difficult. Manuscripts may be known by various and several titles in different languages in different places. Their call numbers may be changed. Even when previously catalogued, items are often incompletely or inaccurately described. Adding to the complexities of dealing with this material is the fact that many large and important collections of Hebrew manuscripts have never been catalogued. Many of these are in Eastern Europe, for example, in Moscow and St. Petersburg, but there are unique collections in the United States and Israel, as well, for which no full description has yet been published. In the United States these include collections at the Jewish Theological Seminary, the Hebrew Union College, and Columbia University. As these collections continue to grow but remain undocumented, increasing numbers of items become inaccessible to scholars, and it becomes ever more difficult, if not impossible, for collectors and dealers to determine the origins of certain works.

The two items listed in Isaia Sonne's catalogue, now in the possession of the Jewish Theological Seminary, however, are cited in Richler's *Corrections and Additions to the Guide to Hebrew Manuscript Collections.*